FIFTY YEARS
THE QUEEN

Princess Elizabeth serving in the Auxiliary Transport Service in World War II.

FIFTY YEARS
THE QUEEN

A TRIBUTE TO HER MAJESTY
QUEEN ELIZABETH II
ON HER GOLDEN JUBILEE

Arthur Bousfield & Garry Toffoli

DUNDURN PRESS
TORONTO AND OXFORD

Publisher: J. Kirk Howard
Design: Heidy Lawrance Associates
Printer: Transcontinental Printing Inc.

Canadian Cataloguing in Publication Data

Bousfield, Arthur, 1943–

Fifty years the queen: a tribute to the Queen on her golden jubilee

ISBN 1-55002-360-8

1. Elizabeth II, Queen of Great Britain, 1926–—Anniversaries, etc. 2. Queens—Great Britain—Biography. I. Toffoli, Garry, 1953–

II. Title.

DA590.B68 2002   941.085'092
C2002-902189-5

1   2   3   4   5   06   05   04   03   02

We acknowledge the support of the *Canada Council for the Arts* and the *Ontario Arts Council* for our publishing program. We also acknowledge the financial support of the *Government of Canada* through the *Book Publishing Industry Development Program* and *The Association for the Export of Canadian Books*, and the *Government of Ontario* through the *Ontario Book Publishers Tax Credit* program.

Care has been taken to trace the ownership of copyright material used in this book. The author and the publisher welcome any information enabling them to rectify any references or credit in subsequent editions.

Printed and bound in Canada. Printed on recycled paper.

www.dundurn.com

Dundurn Press
8 Market Street
Suite 200
Toronto, Ontario, Canada
M5E 1M6

Dundurn Press
73 Lime Walk
Headington, Oxford,
England
OX3 7AD

Dundurn Press
2250 Military Road
Tonawanda NY
U.S.A.
14150

Acknowledgements

In the writing of *Fifty Years The Queen*, the authors owe a great debt of gratitude to Kirk Howard, Chairman, and the other Trustees of the Canadian Royal Heritage Trust/Fonds du patrimoine royal du Canada for allowing them full access to the Trust's important collection of books, pictures, newspapers, scrap books and manuscripts (in particular the Rhea and Ron Anger, M. Ida New and Carl L. Shain collections) and for permitting them to reproduce many items from it. Several volunteer members of the Trust staff also generously assisted them in their work. They would in particular like to acknowledge the help of Claudia Willetts, Trust Librarian; Helen McNeil, Trust Archivist; Charles W. Clark; H. Kent Jackson; Barbara Kemp; Jane Wachna; and W. Mackenzie Youngs. Assistance of the staff of *Monarchy Canada Magazine* is also gratefully recorded.

Permission to use the official Golden Jubilee emblem was graciously given by the Golden Jubilee Office.

As with their previous books, the authors received much help from Richard Toporoski of the University of St Michael's College in matters constitutional, historical and social. Dr Toporoski also allowed them to use some of his pictures. A similar debt is owed to Lisa Mitchell who placed her collection of commemoratives of the Queen at their disposal, photographed the items from it that they chose to use as well as other pieces and assisted them with her extensive knowledge of this field. She also allowed them to use her own pictures of royal tours and royal occasions. For this expenditure of time and effort they are truly grateful.

The authors also wish to thank: John L. Aimers, Dominion Chairman and Founder of The Monarchist League of Canada, for permitting them to reproduce Her Majesty The Queen's approval of the drawing of the League's arms and for other help; Rev'd Harold Logan for supplying a difficult to obtain photograph; Alan Ho, Manager of Motophoto at 2674 Yonge Street, Toronto, for his careful processing of numerous rolls of film; Gordon Schmidt of Hanover for giving permission to reproduce the unique painting of the 1957 opening of Parliament by the Queen which is on loan to the Canadian Royal Heritage Museum at the Diefenbaker Birthplace in Neustadt, Ontario; and H. Kent Jackson for the loan of items from his collection of royal memorabilia.

Illustration Credits

Many of the historical, copyright-expired illustrations and some contemporary illustrations are came from the collection of the Canadian Royal Heritage Trust. The credits for other illustrations are as follows:

Associated Press: 132
Australian High Commission for Canada: 153, 154, 179
Australians for Constitutional Monarchy: 217
Lynne Bell: (*Monarchy Canada* photographer): 168 (top right & bottom right), 169 (bottom left), 170 (bottom left), 190, 196 (top right)
Arthur Bousfield: (*Monarchy Canada* photographer): 40 (bottom), 41, 42, 60, 68 (bottom right), 96 (top left), 96 (bottom left), 97 (middle left), 98 (top left), 114 (top left), 161 (top), 170 (right), 195 (bottom left)
Daphne Bousfield: 97 (bottom right)
British Columbia Government: B. Novak: 180, 181 (top)
British Information Services: 69 (top right), 125, 130, 149, 151, 155, 158, 196 (top left)
Natalie Bullen (*Monarchy Canada* photographer): 137 (left), 169 (top left)
Canadian Chancellery: 146 (bottom left & centre), 147 (top left & centre)
Canadian Heritage: 95 (top right), 119 (right), 146 (top), 165, 225, 226, 228, 229, 230, 231
Canadian Heritage–Victor Pilon: 148 (bottom left), 188, 189 (top & bottom)
Canadian Press: 48 (top right & bottom right), 210
Clara Cirasella (*Monarchy Canada* photographer), 184 (bottom), 195 (bottom right)
Communicate New Zealand: 29 (top right)
Department of National Defence of Canada: 29 (bottom left), 52 (bottom right), 53 (top, middle right), 86, 146 (bottom right), 147 (top right & bottom left)
Derrick Ditchburn: 206
Federal Newsphotos of Canada: 83, 110 (bottom), 115
Jayne Fincher: 213
Jack Fleger: 182
Graphic Industries: 113 (bottom)
House of Commons of Canada: 98 (middle left)
Hudson's Bay Company: 96 (top right)
Janet Huse (*Monarchy Canada* photographer): 29 (middle right & bottom right), 137 (middle right), 168 (left), 201 (top left, top right & bottom right), 202 (left & right), 211 (top), 212, 219
David Levenson: 183 (top & bottom)
Rev'd Harold Logan: 96 (bottom right)
Ashley Lubin (*Monarchy Canada* photographer): 174, 175
Murdoch W. MacLean: 17 (left)
Lisa Mitchell (*Monarchy Canada* photographer): 28 (top left), 52 (middle), 70 (bottom left), 120, 121, 122, 123, 124, 170 (top left), 215, 224 (bottom left)
Monarchist League in Australia & Sir William Dargie: 133
Monarchist League of Canada: 147 (bottom right)
National Archives of Canada: 7, 98 (bottom left), 195 (top right)
National Film Board of Canada: 135, 136 (left), 145 (top & bottom)
National Portrait Gallery: (London) 224 (top left)
New Brunswick Archives: 23 (left)
New Zealand *Herald*: 208
Northwest Territories Government: 141 (right), 196 (bottom right), 207 (top)
Nova Scotia Legislative Library: 97 (top left)
O. P. & F. A.: 137 (bottom)
Charles Pachter: 70 (bottom right)
Photographers International (Terry Fincher): 186, 187
PA News/London Press Service: 28 (bottom left), 181 (bottom), 209 (bottom), 214, 216, 224 (bottom right)
Popperfoto: 116
Prince George *Citizen*: 196 (middle)
Regina *Leader-Post*: 144 (top)
Rogers Communications: 75
Royal Canadian Mounted Police: 223 (bottom right)
Royal Ontario Museum: 17 (right)
Saskatchewan Government: 147 (bottom centre), 172
John Sebert: 18 (bottom)
Beth Solomon (*Monarchy Canada*): 69 (top left)
S. P. G. Archives: 98 (top right)
Sunday Times: 199
Garry Toffoli (*Monarchy Canada* photographer): 28 (top right & middle right), 52 (bottom left & middle right), 53 (bottom right), 156, 157 (top & bottom), 169 (top right & bottom right), 191
Richard Toporoski (*Monarchy Canada* photographer): 29 (top left), 98 (bottom right)
Toronto Archives: 143
Tribune, Nassau: 204
United Press International: 131
United States Information Services: 103
Vancouver *Sun*: 142
White House: 192, 193
Ken Woolley (*Monarchy Canada* photographer): 161 (bottom), 162 (top), 184 (top), 18 5 Jake Wright: 205
Rod Wylie (*Monarchy Canada* photographer): 69 (bottom right)

Table of Contents

Australian portrait of the Queen by Sir William Dargie, featured Her Majesty dressed in the colours of Australia and wearing the wattle flower, the national emblem of the country, on her shoulder.

1

"I Greet You As Your Queen"

Ottawa, 1957

anada is a majestic land! Flanked by the awesomeness of the Atlantic and the Pacific oceans, and crowned by the forbidding and austere beauty of the Arctic, it is embellished by natural jewels of diverse charm. One thinks of the impressive Bedford Basin or the Annapolis Valley fruit orchards, the magnificent St Lawrence River opening the hinterland to the world, or the oceanic proportions of the Great Lakes linked by the thundering roar of the mighty Niagara. There is the austere stone face of the Canadian shield, the haunting vastness of the prairie wheat fields, the aristocratic grandeur of the Rocky Mountains and the lordly rivers that traverse the land. Majestic is the only word that comes close to doing justice to this land.

And what does the land expect of human society? Republicanism is unworthy. No president, elected or appointed, however admirable an individual, could merit governing such a country. Man's response to the land, that is,

the way human society is ordered, must be as majestic as the land itself.

The Great Seal of Canada is the symbol of the Queen's authority and used to authenticate all government documents. Elizabeth II's Great Seal was issued in 1955 and depicts Her Majesty crowned and seated in St Edward's Chair, with her Royal Arms for Canada in front. The Queen exercised her authority in person on the 1957 tour.

God has established a unity between His creations in this world. Only a king or queen, the product of Man's history and God's anointing, can presume to stand before the Canadian land as an equal, to personify the Canadian state and lead the Canadian people. Only a monarchical people, who acknowledge, that while they have power, they are accountable to an authority outside of and above their own will, can comprehend and live with a land that mocks Man's power. Canadians have always been such a people and had such a king or queen.

When the early European explorers landed in Canada they recognised this fact. They gave the land names such as "Kingdom of the Saguenay" and instinctively acknowledged the aboriginal chiefs as "kings".

And the Dominion of the North is at its most majestic in October, when the land dons a multi-coloured mantle of maple brilliance, grander than any mantle imagined by fabled monarchs of antiquity. It beckons its people to celebrate and add to its royal scene.

On an October day in 1957, Monday 14 October—appropriately Thanksgiving Day in Canada that year—Canadians responded to the majesty of God's land with the grandest majesty they could muster around God's anointed. Four short years earlier, on 2 June 1953, Elizabeth II had been anointed and crowned with the title "Queen of Canada" in St Peter's, the ancient Abbey of St Edward the Confessor in Westminster, England. She was the first monarch officially to be crowned with the title "Queen of Canada" and now she was to confirm her title in the Parliament Building of her Canadian realm.

Two days earlier Her Majesty had arrived in

On her arrival in Ottawa the Queen was greeted by Rt Hon. Vincent Massey, the Governor-General. Mr Massey was appointed by the Queen's father, King George VI, just before his death in 1952, and was the first Governor-General of the Queen's reign in Canada. He was also the first Canadian-born Governor-General since the French regime.

Ottawa, capital of Canada and one of the prettiest capitals in the world, transformed by edict of

Queen Victoria a century before from a rough lumbering town into a city of government. Ten thousand had turned out in perfect autumn weather at Uplands Airport to greet their Queen. In a North American combination of egalitarianism and status, the crowds awaited her arrival in temporary bleachers set up at the hanger, as at a football game, but the bleachers were assigned according to rank or position—one for ministers of state and high officials, one for diplomats, and, most importantly, one for school children.

At 4:30 p.m., after a fourteen-hour flight, the British Overseas Airways DC-7C landed at Uplands, and, following a fanfare by the seven Coronation Trumpeters of the Royal Canadian Air Force Central Band, the Queen and Duke of Edinburgh came down the ramp, and Elizabeth II returned as Queen to the country she had left six years before as a Princess.

After being greeted by the Governor-General, Rt Hon. Vincent Massey, and the Prime Minister, Rt Hon. John Diefenbaker and Mrs Diefenbaker and other dignitaries, the royal party left by automobile on the fifteen-mile ride to

The National War Memorial, unveiled by King George VI in 1939, has always been the focus of remembrance in Canada. The Queen laid a special wreath, made by disabled veterans from oak and maple, on her 1957 stay in Ottawa.

Government House (Rideau Hall). It was a slow ride for the streets were lined by 500,000 of the Queen's Canadian subjects, out to welcome her back to her home in the New World.

Rideau Hall was her home, as much as Buckingham Palace in London or Holyroodhouse Palace in Edinburgh. The three services of Canada—the Royal Canadian Navy, the Canadian Army and the Royal Canadian Air Force—took turns mounting guard at her Ottawa residence, and the Royal Canadian Mounted Police would look after escorts and security. A reception at Rideau Hall for the press writers and photographers, the largest number ever to gather for an event in Canada, completed the first day's public activities.

The second day in Canada was a Sunday so, appropriately, it was allocated to remembrance and contemplation. The public day began at 10:00 a.m. when the Queen and Duke laid a wreath at the National War Memorial, as they had done in 1951. The nine-pound wreath had been created by disabled war veterans from the leaves of Canada's history and identity—oak and maple. After the ceremony the royal couple spoke with the veterans—from the two World Wars, the South African War and even from earlier nineteenth century battles. The Duke himself was a veteran of the Second World War.

The ceremony was followed by a Thanksgiving Service at Christ Church Anglican Cathedral. In his sermon the dean of the cathedral spoke of the first thanksgiving in Canada, held by the men of Martin Frobisher's expedition over four hundred years before in the reign of the first Elizabeth, and how the Queen's great-great-uncle, the Marquis of Lorne, as Governor-

General of Canada, had officially proclaimed Thanksgiving a holiday in Canada in 1879.

Ottawa was the scene of the Queen's first ever television broadcast on 13 October. It was delivered in both English and French and was a prelude to her annual TV Christmas broadcasts.

At 9:00 o'clock in the evening Her Majesty was able to bring the spirit of Thanksgiving to all her people in Canada via the innovation of a live television broadcast, prelude to her annual televised Christmas messages that would begin in December. The new medium was supplanting the radio broadcasts which in their turn had supplanted written communications.

In her address the Queen said "I want you to know how happy I am to be in Canada once again, particularly at Thanksgiving", and promised that "one day we shall bring our children here to see this wonderful and exhilarating country". It was a promise that would be fulfilled many times over, not only for her two children of the time but also for her two sons to be born in the next decade.

In the address Her Majesty also described her pride in the diversity of Canada: "Industry and commerce may bring wealth to a country, but the character of a nation is formed by other factors. Race, language, religion, culture and tradition all have some contribution to make, and when I think of the diversity of these factors in Canada today and the achievements that have grown from their union, I feel proud and happy to be Queen of such a nation."

While Sunday was a day for Church, Monday was for State. And a grand day it was. The Fathers of Confederation had declared that the government of Canada was to be carried out by

"Her Majesty personally or by her representative duly authorised". As such a day had been for her father in 1939, this was a day for the new Queen to carry out the government of Canada personally. The Governor-General, Vincent Massey recalled,

During my time in Ottawa everything possible was done to bring home the position of the Sovereign in our national life. The Queen's visit in 1957 gave this reality. When she opened Parliament, she was acting, in the fullest sense, as the Queen of Canada. At this time she presided over a meeting of her Canadian Privy Council and in her capacity as Sovereign approved an order-in-council.

I cannot claim any personal credit for these arrangements because they were the result of government decisions, but within the limits of my post I was happy to give them the fullest encouragement. I may say

The Queen and members of the Queen's Privy Council for Canada, including the Duke of Edinburgh (to the Queen's left), who was admitted to the Council at this meeting, and the Prime Minister, John Diefenbaker (to the Queen's Right), gather at Rideau Hall for a meeting chaired by the Queen.

this: both the governments [Liberal and Conservative] that were successively in office during my time were at one in their desire that we should demonstrate in every possible way the fact that the Queen is Queen of Canada. There was never the slightest shadow of disagreement on this vital principle.

Massey's point was well made. It was the Liberal government of the venerable monarchist Louis St-Laurent which had initiated the Queen's tour. In the 1957 general election the Liberals were unexpectedly defeated, and now it was the Conservatives under the dynamic and charismatic monarchist John Diefenbaker who carried it out.

The meeting of the Queen's Privy Council for Canada took place at 10:00 a.m. at Government House on that historic Thanksgiving Day, chaired by Her Majesty The Queen. Some voices had suggested that it was not correct British constitutional practice, for a monarch to chair a Privy Council meeting, but Diefenbaker saw the larger principle of identifying the Queen with the workings of her Canadian government and brushed aside such pedantry. As there was no constitutional prohibition, the Queen would chair the Council. Mr Diefenbaker added that "The Queen of Canada is a term which we like to use because it utterly represents her role on this occasion".

Mr Diefenbaker also used the occasion to honour the Duke of Edinburgh. In February of 1957 the Queen had made the Duke a Prince of the United Kingdom, restoring the dignity of "Prince" which he had given up in 1947 as a

Prince of Greece and Denmark. On 3 February 1953, during discussion of the Queen's new Royal Style and Title for Canada in the House of Commons, an opposition M.P. from Lake Centre named John Diefenbaker had suggested that "we should make Her Majesty acquainted with the fact that we as her subjects in Canada would like to see her consort, Prince Philip, the Duke of Edinburgh, created a prince of the Commonwealth to bind us together ever closer in heart and soul and to have in him as in her a link with all parts of the Commonwealth". It was an imaginative idea that, although not adopted, in fact described the life that lay before the consort of the Queen. Now, as the Canadian Prime Minister, John Diefenbaker was able to advise Her Majesty to grant a Canadian honour to the Prince by admitting him to the Queen's Privy Council for Canada. The Prince was duly sworn in that morning, taking his oath before his Canadian Queen.

Prince Philip was also honoured that morning by becoming an Honorary Fellow of the Royal Society of Canada, the organisation established by the Marquis of Lorne, who was also the Prince's great-great-uncle as well as the Queen's. This event took place at Government House following the Privy Council meeting, as did the reception for the heads of Commonwealth and foreign diplomatic missions and their wives.

At 2:30 p.m., in brilliant autumn sunshine, a procession left Rideau Hall. Modest in scale by British standards perhaps, the procession was still glorious in appearance by any standard. Leading and following the state landau were contingents of the Royal Canadian Mounted

Police—48 in all—in their famous scarlet serge tunics, blue breeches and tan stetsons, riding noble coal-black horses, with red and white pennons fluttering from the upright lances in their right hands. Their predecessors had brought the Queen's Peace to the West, now they were bringing the Queen herself to Parliament.

The open maroon landau with the Royal Arms emblazoned on the sides was a gift to Canada from Earl Grey, Governor-General of Canada 1904 to 1910. He had brought it with him from Australia where it had been made. It was Lord Grey who had coined the expression "the Maple Crown" to describe the Canadian Monarchy, and it seemed an apt phrase as the

The Queen and Duke of Edinburgh proceed through the gothic halls of the Canadian Parliament led by the Gentleman Usher of the Black Rod and followed by John Diefenbaker.

Queen rode in his landau while the sun lit up the maple trees of Ottawa in their fall colour.

But most splendid of all was the figure riding in the landau. The Queen was resplendent in her Coronation gown, embroidered with the rose of England, the thistle of Scotland, the shamrock of Ireland and the leek of Wales, the wattle flower of Australia, the fern of New Zealand, the protea of South Africa, an ear of wheat for Pakistan, the lotus flowers for India and Ceylon and, in green silk bordered with gold bullion thread and veined in crystal, the maple leaves of Canada. In her hair Her Majesty wore a tiara that had been a silver wedding gift to Queen Alexandra and had also been worn by Queen Mary, who bequeathed it to Elizabeth II. The dress provided a deliberate symbolic link between the Coronation ceremony and the parliamentary one.

Past thousands of cheering Canadians the procession travelled the traditional route along Sussex Drive and Wellington Street to Parliament Hill, where the largest crowd ever seen on the hill had gathered. The Queen was en route to open the twenty-third Parliament, the first monarch to open a Canadian Parliament in person.

Once inside the gothic halls of Parliament—Westminster in the Wilderness it had been dubbed in the previous century—the party

Painting by Guy Laliberté depicts the Queen reading the Speech from the Throne as she becomes the first monarch to open the Canadian Parliament in person. Her Majesty sits on the Throne of Canada with the Duke of Edinburgh on the Consort's Throne and the Prime Minister, John Diefenbaker on a chair to the Queen's right. The painting belongs to Gordon Schmidt of Hanover, Ontario and is displayed at the Canadian Royal Heritage Museum located in the birthplace of John Diefenbaker in Neustadt, Ontario.

was led at a dignified pace by the Gentleman Usher of the Black Rod. Accompanied by her consort and attended by the Prime Minister, the Leader of the Senate and military officers, the Queen reached the red Senate Chamber and proceeded up the centre aisle past the senators and invited diplomats and guests and past the scarlet and ermine robed justices of the Supreme Court. She then ascended the low dais and occupied the Throne of Canada.

When the Commons had attended at the Bar of the Senate, Her Majesty addressed the Senate and Commons in the Speech from the Throne opening the new Parliament: "I greet you as your Queen, together we constitute the Parliament of Canada." She concluded her speech by recalling the words of the first Elizabeth, "'Though God hath raised me high, yet this I count the glory of my crown, that I have reigned with your loves.' And now, in the New World I say to you that it is my wish that in the years before me I may so reign in Canada and be so remembered."

It was an historic moment in the story of Canada and the life of Her Majesty—the Queen in Parliament, but all such moments are both the beginning of new chapters and the continuation of earlier episodes in the life of both Queen and Country.

Even the tour itself was not yet complete. Still to come was the evening's reception at Rideau Hall when the Queen donned the famous "Maple Leaf Dress", further emphasising her status as a Canadian Queen. Tuesday was devoted to civic events in both Ottawa and Hull, such as launching the construction of the new Queensway expressway through Ottawa.

These events were attended by hundreds of thousands of people on both sides of the provincial border between Ontario and Quebec, which Ottawa and Hull straddle. There was also a surprise gift for the Queen at dinner that evening.

A 350-pound sturgeon had been caught off Nova Scotia—the first in ten years. By ancient law, all sturgeons caught in the waters of the Queen's realms belong to the Sovereign, so the fish was packed in ice and flown to Rideau Hall by the Royal Canadian Air Force, where, that evening, it was presented to Her Majesty.

Wednesday morning there was time for an assembly of 15,000 school children at Lansdowne Park before a departure for the United States. Of the trip to Canada's southern neighbour and other travels around the world, the Queen assured Canadians that her role as Queen of Canada did not arbitrarily end at Canada's border. "When you hear or read about the events in Washington, and other places, I want you to reflect that it is the Queen of Canada and her husband who are concerned in them", she said.

And the 1957 tour was but the first of many for Elizabeth II as Queen of Canada, in a reign that would see, and continues to see, many changes in Her Majesty's life, her role as Queen, and in the countries over which she reigns. Nor did the Queen's involvement in Canadian life and Canadians involvement in her life begin in 1957. There had been the Coronation, the 1951 tour as Princess and her years of preparation for the Throne. It was a throne which, at her birth, only a few expected would be hers to inherit.

The largest crowd ever seen on Parliament Hill watches as the royal couple depart in the state landau of Canada, escorted by the Royal Canadian Mounted Police.

The famous "maple leaf dress" worn by the Queen at the reception in Rideau Hall is now one of the treasures of the Canadian Museum of Civilization in Ottawa.

Accompanied by Vincent Massey, and led by one of the Governor-General's dogs, the Queen walks through the leaf-covered grounds of Rideau Hall. The Duke of Edinburgh is to the right of the picture.

The Queen, the American President Dwight Eisenhower, Mamie Eisenhower and the Duke of Edinburgh pose at a reception in Washington. The visit to the United States emphasised the ties of friendship between the two North American countries of the Queen and the President. "When you hear or read about the events in Washington and other places, I want you to reflect that it is the Queen of Canada and her husband who are concerned in them", Her Majesty said before flying to Washington.

Continuing a tradition in the grounds of her Canadian home, Rideau Hall, the Queen plants a tree. She had also planted a tree in 1951 and her father, King George VI had planted one in 1939.

2

"Lilibet"

1926–1936

The Landor portrait of the baby Princess Elizabeth in her mother's arms, painted before Christmas 1926.

Queen Elizabeth II was just 31 that mellow autumn day in 1957 when she first occupied her Canadian Throne in her High Court of Parliament. Life had begun for her on a drizzly spring day only three decades before. The eventual holder of many titles made her debut in history as simply Her Royal Highness Princess Elizabeth of York. The place of her birth was 17 Bruton Street, the London town house of her maternal grandparents, the Earl and Countess of Strathmore and Kinghorne; the date Wednesday, 21 April 1926; the time 2:40 a.m.

Canadians read about the royal birth that day in their evening papers or heard the news by radio if they had one. "Daughter Is Born To Duchess Of York" the front page of the Toronto *Globe* announced. *The Toronto Daily Star*, knowing its readers' great interest in royalty, carried a fuller report. The baby's mother it revealed had "always loved children". The infant's paternal grandmother had spent weeks "selecting baby

Princess Elizabeth's greatest gift at birth was the parents she received. The Duke and Duchess of York were a devoted couple determined to create a happy family life for themselves and their children.

clothes, buying miniature toilet articles and powder boxes and even with her own hand fashioning delicate coverlets for the baby's crib". An especially nice touch, the paper felt, were the "numerous sheafs of daffodils from the humbler folk" among the mass of floral gifts to the Duchess from the high born and famous.

Who was this new Princess and what would be her destiny? Her identity was simple. Princess Elizabeth was the first child of Their Royal Highnesses the Duke and Duchess of York. Her father the Duke was Prince Albert— 'Bertie' to his family. He was second son of the world's greatest reigning monarch, King George V, Sovereign of the global British Empire and its self-governing Dominions—namely Canada, Australia, South Africa, New Zealand, Newfoundland and the Irish Free State—and Emperor of India, who had been on the Throne since 1910. The new Princess was third in line to this splendid and ancient Crown after her uncle the Prince of Wales and her father.

"Nobody thought she would one day become Queen" writes a biographer of Elizabeth II. In fact, accounts of her birth indicate just such a possibility did occur to some at the time. Taking its lead from the United Kingdom papers, the *Toronto Daily Star* noted "there is a possibility that today's baby may become…sovereign". In its second report the next day it informed readers that the new Princess would likely be called Elizabeth. "Elizabeth" it said "makes a strong appeal to the popular imagination because of the possibility of the little newcomer some day ascending the throne" and bringing "another Elizabethan era".

Such predictions were not wild ones. In the past two hundred years the Crown had sometimes failed to go from father to son. When a monarch was childless it had passed to a brother. From George III's family it had been transmitted to his fourth son's only child, Queen Victoria. Victoria's eldest son in turn was succeeded, not by his first born son but by his second. The chance that Princess Elizabeth's dashing, popular bachelor uncle the Prince of Wales, Heir to the Throne,—the family knew him as David—might never marry was already in people's minds. "It has become common to assume the continued bachelordom of the Prince of Wales" the *Toronto Daily Star* hinted portentously.

The idea that the baby Princess Elizabeth might wear the Crown was no solemn prophecy. Even those who thought about it clearly did not anticipate it could be before she reached middle age. Still, the notion remained in the public mind. The next few years would decide. Most assumed the Princess's young parents, the Duke and Duchess of York, would have more children. If they did, one would likely be a son. Sons took their place ahead of daughters in the order of succession, so Princess Elizabeth in that case would go down to fourth spot or lower.

And the subject of all this conjecture? Princess Elizabeth was a healthy baby with a well-shaped head and tiny ears. She had fair hair, a lovely complexion and "large dark lashed blue eyes". Her grandmother Queen Mary found her "enchanting". Her birth had been a difficult one by Caesarean section. In the 1920s that was not openly discussed but the media conveyed the fact nonetheless, telling readers that "special gynaecological treatment had to be adopted". It was a good sign for her future that the Princess made her first impact on the world just by arriving in it. Her birth was twelve days before the British General Strike which threatened to engulf the centre of the Empire in bitter class warfare. Joy over the birth of the Princess relieved the tension and caused a temporary drop in the number of reported subversive incidents.

King George V readily approved the names Elizabeth Alexandra Mary for his new granddaughter when submitted to him by her father. The first, Elizabeth, was the name of her mother the Duchess of York. A favourite pastime of the Duchess as a child had been dressing up in romantic costumes at her family's historic Glamis Castle. On one unforgettable occasion, arrayed as the seventeenth century Princess Elizabeth—the 'Winter Queen' of Bohemia, daughter of King James I—she danced a set with her youngest brother to entertain guests there. Elizabeth had fond associations for her. Alexandra was the name of George V's beloved mother, the beautiful though sad Queen Alexandra, who had died the previous year. Mary was of course for his wife, Queen Mary, the child's paternal grandmother.

Water from the River Jordan was procured for the baptism of the five-week old Princess Elizabeth on 29 May in the private chapel of Buckingham Palace. Dressed in a cream Brussels

Elizabeth's father's family was the most famous family in the world—the Royal Family of the Commonwealth of Nations. This picture taken at the time of World War I shows them together except for the eldest son the Prince of Wales who was absent at the Front serving with the Canadian Expeditionary Force. From left: Duke of York; Prince George (Duke of Kent); Queen Mary; Prince Henry (Duke of Gloucester); King George V; and Princess Mary (Princess Royal). Princess Elizabeth quickly became the darling of her formidable grandparents King George V and Queen Mary, bringing joy into their lives and evoking a somewhat uncharacteristic affection from them in return.

lace gown, the baby cried throughout the ceremony. She had to be given an old pacifier for babies—a dose of dill water. On her behalf, six godfathers and godmothers made the first of many promises in her life, pledging the small Princess to "obediently keep God's holy will and commandments, and walk in the same" all the days of her life. One godfather represented the oldest generation of the Royal Family. He was Elizabeth's great-great uncle, the Duke of Connaught, who had been Governor-General of Canada from 1911 to 1916.

The new Princess possessed a glorious heritage. The royal line she was born into was that of the legends of King Arthur, Saxon Common Law, Shakespeare's kings and queens and the Crown in Parliament. Yet the range and diversity of her gene pool always surprises people who think of Elizabeth II in a limiting way as "English" or "British". On her father's side, her family had recently—in 1917—adopted the name Windsor to make their German origin less offensive in wartime. Her paternal grandmother was a Danish Princess. Farther back the roots were more multicultural—even multiracial. French, Spanish, Italian, Portuguese, Polish, Cuman, Norwegian, Swedish and Flemish, as well as Dutch, Lithuanian, English, Arab, Byzantine Greek, Georgian, Armenian, Serbian and Welsh, were some of those to be found. Her ancestors belonging to those cultures (and others) included kings, queens, princes, princesses, saints, conquerors, warriors, statesmen, diplomats, law-givers, churchmen and patrons of the arts. Her lineage was a pathway through history. Coming partly from the international character of royalty, partly from the

As a princess, Elizabeth possessed ancestors in abundance, but the diversity of her roots is not really appreciated. Her forebears in fact were not only international but also interracial. Through her grandmother Queen Mary, for example, one ancestral line leads back to Genghis Khan

multi-ethnic composition of the United Kingdom, it was the right background for someone who would reign over multicultural countries in a multiracial Commonwealth.

There were many religions represented in it too: pagans, Jews, Christians and Muslims. And of course plenty of rogues as well as heroes. Surprisingly, the staid Queen Mary provided her granddaughter Elizabeth with an exotic strain close to hand. The Consort of George V was the granddaughter of a beautiful, tragic Hungarian, Countess Claudine de Rhédey de Kis-Rhéde, whose bloodline included—besides Hungarians, Croatians and Khazars—the mighty Genghis Khan himself, a grandson of whom, Kublai Khan, became Emperor of China. Another unexpected ancestral twist was not too remote either. Princess Elizabeth's great-great-great-great grandmother Queen Charlotte, wife of King George III,—the Queen after whom Charlottetown, capital of Prince Edward Island, is named—is thought to have had Black ancestry and has been claimed by the Black community as a link to the Royal Family.

The well-known Scottish heritage of Princess

Princess Elizabeth's great-great-great-great grandmother Queen Charlotte, depicted in this portrait in the New Brunswick Legislature, had Black ancestors.

intensely blue eyes". Her daughter most certainly inherited the blue eyes.

Whatever ancestral genes predominate in a child, the role of the parents is decisive. Here Princess Elizabeth was exceptionally fortunate. Her father, the Duke of York, was good looking and intelligent, a decent and courageous man. He had a strong though not fully developed character. Unfortunately he also suffered from shyness, a certain lack of self-esteem and an unfortunate upbringing that had left him with a pronounced stammer. Princess Elizabeth's mother, the Duchess, formerly Lady Elizabeth Bowes-Lyon, had as the *Toronto Daily Star* pointed out gained the name "the smiling Duchess". In barely three years of marriage to the Duke of York she, by her graciousness, reversed Queen Victoria's rigid rule that the Royal Family should always appear looking serious in public so as not to be thought frivolous. And the public applauded the change.

Princess Elizabeth's maternal grandparents, the Earl and Countess of Strathmore and Kinghorne, portrayed here with their ten children in the drawing room of their ancient seat Glamis Castle, were Scottish nobles who might have stepped out of a Scott novel. Public spirited, good landlords, devoutly Episcopalian and steeped in Jacobite tradition, they were hospitable, fun loving, musical and closely knit as a family.

Elizabeth's mother, which was to be a lasting influence on her, has tended to overshadow the important strain of native Irish ancestry—an ironic endowment given the continuing Irish problem—she also inherited on the maternal side. The Duchess's mother was a direct descendant of Red Hugh O'Neill, last native King of Ulster. Not only was this Irish ancestry more recent, it was also visible. The old Minister of Glamis recalled that the Duchess as a young girl had "the traditional Irish blend of dark hair and

In her person the Duchess of York was beautiful and elegant. Born with a quick intelligence, remarkable self possession and lack of self consciousness, she was also endowed with a rare kindness, common sense and genuine interest in others. These qualities had flourished in the happy environment created by her fond parents and nine brothers and sisters. She and the Duke were moreover very much in love.

Both parents welcomed Princess Elizabeth's birth. "We always wanted a child to make our happiness complete" the Duke wrote to his mother, Queen Mary, a few days after the event. They were determined to create a happy home life for their daughter—the Duchess because she had so much loved her own family, the Duke because he yearned for the satisfactory family life he had not had as a child.

But it was not to be quite yet. Soon after Princess Elizabeth was born she was called on for the first of a lifetime of sacrifices to that insatiable deity—royal duty. She found her parents suddenly snatched from her. The Duke and Duchess of York were told by the King that they must undertake a six-month tour of Australia and New Zealand, a tour the Prince of Wales was supposed to have made.

The Duke and Duchess sailed for the Antipodes in January 1927. "It quite broke me up" wrote the Duchess at having to leave her baby. In their absence, care of their nine-month-old daughter was shared between the two sets of grandparents, the Strathmores and King George V and Queen Mary. When their turn came, the elderly Sovereigns who had not had much empathy with their own children were captivated by Princess Elizabeth. They developed an immediate rapport with their grand-

The Princess at 2. A portrait photograph by Marcus Adams hand coloured in pastel. The pose suggests a modern version of a Renaissance cherub.

daughter, doting on her, spoiling her. But the absence of Elizabeth's parents was a long one. When the Duke and Duchess came back from their highly successful tour, the Princess did not recognise them.

The day of the Yorks' return, 27 June, the Duke and Duchess appeared on the balcony of Buckingham Palace and Princess Elizabeth, now a year and two months old, was held up under an umbrella for the first time to the cheering crowds below. Family life was resumed. The Yorks now had a house of their own: 145 Piccadilly, a tall, narrow, austere looking building topped with a dome and not far from the Palace. Princess Elizabeth's nursery was at the top of the house. It was presided over by her nanny Clara Knight who had been nanny to the Duchess when she was a baby. Unable to say Clara, the Princess called her Ah-lah. She also invented a name for herself. Trying to pronounce Elizabeth, she came out with Lilibet. When she went to stay with George V at Bognor, where he was convalescing in the wake of a serious illness in 1929, her grandfather began calling her Lilibet. The name was adopted by the rest of the Royal Family.

Joined with Mrs Knight in the care of the Princess were Margaret—called Bobo—and Ruby, the MacDonald sisters, daughters of a Scottish railway worker. Bobo was first nursemaid then dresser to Princess Elizabeth while Ruby was subsequently attached in the same capacity to Princess Margaret, Elizabeth's sister. For Bobo it was to be a lifetime of service and friendship with Elizabeth II.

Princess Elizabeth also acquired two other homes. Birkhall on the Balmoral estate was assigned to the Yorks as a holiday residence. More important for her was Royal Lodge, a somewhat derelict hunting lodge that had belonged to George IV in Windsor Great Park, near enough to the Castle for convenience but sufficiently secluded to ensure complete privacy. The Yorks altered the Gothic style structure, added new wings and together created a

The Hungarian Philip de Laszlo, one of the 20ᵗʰ century's great portrait painters, captured Princess Elizabeth at 7 with his customary style and elegance.

beautiful garden in the grounds. The family moved there in 1932 using Royal Lodge as their weekend country house. It was painted pink to recall the rose colour brick of the Duchess' childhood home St Paul's Walden Bury. They made it a charming residence and today it is still the home of Elizabeth II's mother Queen Elizabeth The Queen Mother at age 101.

The Princess grew rapidly. Winston Churchill met her in 1928 when she was two and a half and found her "a character". "She has" he wrote his wife "an air of authority and reflectiveness astonishing in an infant". The Princess was a good child: quiet, obedient, kind and unselfish, though she did not and would never possess the spontaneous charm her mother had at a similar

1933 Newfoundland stamp showing Princess Elizabeth at 5.

25

Y Bwthyn Bach or The Little House, a miniature thatched cottage eleven feet high in the garden of Royal Lodge, was given to Princess Elizabeth by the people of Wales on her sixth birthday in 1931. The Little House was fully equipped and in it Her Royal Highness learned the rudiments of housework.

age, the charm that with a glance captures the devotion of an individual or a crowd for life. Princess Elizabeth was also affectionate and good natured.

The year of her fourth birthday—1930—was a milestone. For her birthday she received her first pony—Peggy—from King George V. He was the person who awakened in her a passionate love of horses. The same year her sister Margaret was born. "I've got a baby sister, Margaret Rose, and I'm going to call her Bud" Elizabeth confided to a friend of her Mother. "Why Bud?" asked the friend. "Well, she's not a real Rose yet, is she? She's only a Bud" replied the logical Princess. There was surprise and disappointment that the new child was a daughter not a son. Princess Elizabeth's place in the succession was not only unshaken, the continued bachelorhood of the Prince of Wales focused public attention more and more on her. For the first time the Duke of York, discussing how his daughter resembled the young Queen Victoria with his friend Osbert Sitwell, expressed the thought that Elizabeth might become Queen.

She was in fact the most famous child in the world. At three she appeared on the cover of *Time*—as a fashion trendsetter. People had found she wore yellow dresses and so all over the world little girls were dressed in yellow. When she was four a wax figure of her mounted on a pony was added to the famous Madam Tussaud's Museum. Her precocious personality began to be known throughout her grandfather's far flung realms. Looking back from the world of instant communications it is hard to imagine just how the character of a four-year-old communicated itself to people so far away. But in addition to the general interest aroused by royalty, Princess Elizabeth fulfilled a yearning the public felt for the wholesomeness of children and family, a need born of the horrors of the First World War and the perceived disintegration of society in the wake of the conflict.

In some respects Princess Elizabeth became better known than her parents. At least for the peoples and parts of the Empire where the Yorks had not been seen. Her small person interested adults as well as the children who were in age her peers. Pictures were taken of her by the London children's photographer Marcus Adams, who had a rapidly growing reputation in the field, so her parents could keep up with her growth when they were in Australia and New Zealand. Once released to the public the photos became incredibly popular and found their way everywhere.

A small provincial newspaper, *The Evening Examiner* in Peterborough, Ontario, for example, published a picture of Princess Elizabeth in its 31 March 1930 issue, a month prior to her fourth birthday. The accompanying story told how the Photographers' Association of America decided to hold contests to discover the most attractive child "in America and Ontario, respectively". To arouse interest in the contests, Charles Ashley, President of the Ontario Photographers' Association, telephoned Marcus Adams to ask for the loan of some portraits

As she grew, the Princess developed a close relationship with her father. Here is her father's delightful snapshot of the happy Princess at 4 among the lilies of Royal Lodge.

THE HOUSES OF WINDSOR

As the Queen of 16 realms, Elizabeth II has official residences throughout the world, where she stays when carrying out her duties in person. Unlike her representatives, who occupy them for only a few years, Her Majesty has made them her homes for more than fifty years, and her ancestors and relatives called them home decades and centuries earlier. They are truly the Houses of Windsor.

Buckingham Palace, the Queen's London residence.

Windsor Castle, just outside of London, is the weekend home of the Royal Family, and gave the family its name.

In Scotland the Queen's home is Holyroodhouse Palace in Edinburgh.

The Royal Yacht BRITANNIA was the home shared by the whole Commonwealth, as it travelled to many lands to provide a residence for the Queen and the Royal Family. Here it is seen in the Bahamas.

When in Canadian waters the BRITANNIA flew the Queen's Canadian Banner and the Canadian National Flag.

Yarralumla, in Canberra, Australia has welcomed the Queen several times.

The New Zealand Government House in Wellington, the Queen's residence in that Pacific land, is a large, two-storeyed wooden house with attics and a flag turret, built in 1910.

In Quebec City, the ancient capital of Canada, the Queen and Governor-General stay at a special residence inside the old Citadel fortress.

Rideau Hall, in Ottawa, a rambling residence much added to over the decades, has been the Royal Family's Canadian address since 1865. Based on a house dating from 1838, the front facade, created in 1913, bears a resemblance to Buckingham Palace, whose facade was added at about the same time. The garden front has the intimacy of a country home. Rideau Hall first became the Queen's home in 1951, when she was a Princess.

Right: Princess Elizabeth with her father and sister on horseback in Windsor Great Park.

of royal children. Ashley knew his fellow Canadians' interest in the Royal Family and how fascinated Americans also found them. Marcus Adams sent Ashley his latest studies of Princess Elizabeth.

The Marcus Adams photos thus found their way into *The Evening Examiner*, the first headed "Study of Princess Elizabeth". The paper published another portrait photo on 29 April—Princess Elizabeth with Queen Mary. The first picture carried a short story about the Princess, perhaps true, perhaps apocryphal, which showed her as a natural, endearing child. "The little princess" it ran "recently discovered, in Buckingham Palace yard, that every time she passed the guardsman in sentry-go, he presented arms to her. And before the nursemaid discovered the situation had run the poor fellow nearly ragged". Stories like this not only

appeared in newspapers. About this time G. Howard Ferguson, Premier of Ontario, addressed the Empire Club of Canada, a noted dining club for prominent professionals and businessmen, and is recorded as having begun his talk with anecdotes about the Royal Family.

Princess Elizabeth's life settled into a pattern. Easter was spent at Windsor Castle with the King and Queen. In August and September she visited her grandparents, the Strathmores at Glamis Castle and the King and Queen at Balmoral. Christmas meant going to Sandringham. The rest of the time was divided between 145 Piccadilly and Royal Lodge. Her love of horses and country life continued to increase. In the hall outside her nursery at 145 Piccadilly she kept a "stable" of thirty to forty toy horses and unsaddled them all every night. At five she began formal riding lessons with Owen, the

In 1930 Princess Elizabeth acquired a special responsibility, a sister to look after, Princess Margaret, born that year at Glamis Castle. Here the royal sisters are 6 and 2 respectively.

began for the Princess. Marion Crawford's account of her seventeen years with Princess Elizabeth and Princess Margaret was published as *The Little Princesses* in 1950. By writing the book the author violated the trust and friendship of the Royal Family so her memoir created a minor scandal. Its contents on the other hand in no way merited the uproar. Quite the contrary, they confirmed that the future Elizabeth II had enjoyed just the happy family life the public imagined.

Marion Crawford was a product of the Moray House Training College in Edinburgh and intended to become a child psychologist.

royal groom, at White Lodge, Windsor. Princess Elizabeth's favourite games all involved playing at horses. She sought every book she could find on the subject, watched the drayhorses delivering goods in the streets below her nursery windows and counted the days to the annual Horse Show at Olympia. She announced she was going to marry a farmer in order to have lots of cows, horses and dogs.

The year 1932 ushered in another phase of Elizabeth's development. In the spring Crawfie arrived as her governess and serious schooling

Riding her tricycle. Despite the world's keen interest in her, Princess Elizabeth had a normal and relatively private upbringing.

With her grand-mother Queen Mary who took a close interest in the Princess's education, arranging excursions to museums, historic sites and concerts with her.

hour lessons began. At the start of the week, the first period was devoted to religious instruction, other days to arithmetic. Four periods were allotted to history, two to grammar, one each to literature, writing, composition, poetry and geography. A break of an hour followed at 11:00 with orange juice and play time. Twelve to one was time for reading, half for silent reading and half with Miss Crawford reading aloud. Lunch took place at one o'clock. The afternoon was taken up with singing (the Princess had a good voice), dancing, music and drawing until 4:45 when there was tea. The evening meal was at 7:15 p.m., followed by bathtime.

Princess Elizabeth saw her parents in the morning before lessons, lunched with them if they were at home, spent the hour from 5:30 to 6:30 p.m. with them and was visited by them when having her bath—a happy time of noisy splashing and general fun. So close a relationship between parents and children was unusual in any family of the time that could afford a staff of servants. It surprised and pleased Crawfie.

She had taught underprivileged children in the Scottish capital and knew the latest methods of progressive nursery teaching. She was a person of great energy. Her prowess at walking had been what first impressed the Duke of York. On arriving in the Yorks household she was astounded at the freedom Princess Elizabeth's parents allowed her. They "were not over concerned with the higher education of their daughters" she recalled. "They wanted most for them a really happy childhood, with lots of pleasant memories stored up against the days that might come out and, later, happy marriages".

Crawfie, as Princess Elizabeth promptly named her, set up a six-day weekly programme of instruction for her nearly six-year-old charge. Her Royal Highness woke at 7:30 a.m. and had breakfast. She went downstairs at 9:00 and half

As the head gardener (left) gives advice, Princess Elizabeth (fourth from left) plants a tree at a birthday party for her second cousin the Master of Carnegie (third from right) in the Garden of Friendship.

Crawfie found Princess Elizabeth could already read. She had been taught by her mother at five just as the Duchess had been by hers. Bible stories, *Alice, Black Beauty, At The Back Of The North Wind, Peter Pan* were the books she began with. The new governess also discovered what her pupil was like. Princess Elizabeth had a high I.Q. and was an unusually observant child who at their first meeting noticed the governess's uncommon hair style. She was very self disciplined and had almost a passion for order. Even better "there was always about her a certain amenability, a reasonableness rare in anyone so very young". Nor did it take long to discover Elizabeth's strong relationship with her father or see that she had inherited his shyness and tendency to take things seriously. Also like the Duke, Princess Elizabeth found it hard to express her emotions. She did not give her love and affection easily but when she did they were given permanently.

The education of Elizabeth II and her sister Princess Margaret at home not at a school with other children has been strongly criticised. Crawfie later wrote that it seemed to her that "in those days we lived in an ivory tower, removed from the real world". This isolation has been exagger-

ated. Elizabeth and her sister Margaret, when the latter joined the nursery, did see other children. Tea time was when youngsters their own age were invited—relatives or the children of friends and members of the household. Elizabeth and her sister also went to children's parties. Crawfie's attempt to initiate more outside contacts failed dismally. On a visit to the YWCA the two Princesses were recognised and mobbed and rides on top of a double-decker

At her studies. Elizabeth was precocious and hardworking in the schoolroom.

bus had to cease when the IRA began a letter box bomb campaign. But even without these external contacts Crawfie had to admit that her pupils "were two entirely normal and healthy

There were of course many occasions for boisterous high spirits too.

little girls, and we had our difficulties. Neither was above taking a whack at her adversary, if roused, and Lilibet was quick with her left hook!"

Of all the family, Queen Mary took the closest interest in the intellectual content of Elizabeth's educational programme. She arranged for her granddaughter to have a professional governess, Mrs Montaudon-Smith, to teach her French so that lessons would not be interrupted by Crawfie's holidays. The Princess responded well and became perfectly fluent in a language vitally important in her eventual capacity as Queen of Canada. (Her studies in French were later taken to a more advanced level by Vicomtesse Antoinette de Bellaigue.) Queen Mary also felt that more school room time should be devoted to history and had royal genealogies added to the curriculum. She made sure both granddaughters were thoroughly taught the geography of the Dominions. For

Elizabeth's fourth birthday she gave her a set of building blocks made of fifty different woods from around the Commonwealth, maple from Canada, teak from Malaya and so on. The classics of literature were regular gifts from her to her granddaughter. She arranged her own outings—more successfully than Crawfie—for the two Princesses: regular cultural visits to museums, art galleries and historic sites.

Noticing Princess Elizabeth was bored during a performance at Queen's Hall, Queen Mary asked if she would like to go home. "Oh no, Granny" replied Elizabeth, "we can't leave before the end. Think of all the people who'll be waiting to see us outside". Her grandmother promptly had her taken away unseen and sent home in a taxi. This was education of a different kind than governesses provided but just as essential for the Princess. The lesson, as Robert Lacey who tells the story in *Majesty* points out, was that "being royal was a matter of living out a role, not acting it". Princess Elizabeth had now also taken on a responsibility. Integration of her young sister Margaret into family life brought out the protective side of her. Margaret was an amusing extrovert. She needed a good example and had to be saved from the consequences of her own folly when she got into scrapes. This helped Elizabeth grow up too.

Princess Elizabeth's first five years coincided with developments in family and state that settled in advance the framework of her future life and role as Queen. Six months after her birth, her father followed his wife's advice to make one more attempt—his tenth—to overcome his serious speech problem. On 19 October 1926 accompanied by the Duchess, he made his way to the consulting rooms of Lionel Logue, an Australian speech therapist practicing in London. Daily visits and home breathing exercises followed. The skilful Logue gave his patient hope. Prince Bertie's speech, marred by stuttering, long pauses and the inability to say certain words, slowly showed noticeable improvement. He began to feel confident about the six-month Australian and New Zealand tour that lay ahead. Of more lasting importance, his cure released the latent qualities necessary to the full development of his character. Had this not happened, it is doubtful whether he would have felt able to accept the Crown when it fell to his lot. The other family development was less happy. Princess Elizabeth's uncle David continued unwed, growing daily more bored with his job as Heir to the Throne.

The year 1926 also saw the Balfour Declaration on the status of the Dominions. The second British Empire—the first ended with the defection of the Americans in 1775–1783—came together haphazardly, almost reluctantly, and reached its greatest territorial extent following World War I. Larger components of the Empire—Canada for instance in 1867, Australia in 1901, South Africa in 1910—developed self-government and regional union. But was the Empire's destiny to be complete independence of its parts or federation with an Imperial Parliament and Imperial Government? The debate raged for years. If anything, voices for federation were louder from the overseas provinces than

from the United Kingdom and in the end it was the British electorate that rejected federation. The Dominions meanwhile had built up sophisticated domestic economies making that option unlikely anyway. World War I spurred the growth of nationalism—Canada certainly felt the stir of nationhood with the sacrifice its troops made to win the desperate victory of Vimy Ridge in 1917—and political independence carried the day.

At the Imperial Conference held in early November 1926, a committee of the Dominion Prime Ministers headed by the former United Kingdom Prime Minister, Earl Balfour, defined what a Dominion was. "They are autonomous communities within the British Empire" it declared, "equal in status, in no way subordinate one to another in any aspect of their domestic or external affairs though united by a common allegiance to the Crown, and freely associated as members of the British Commonwealth of Nations". It took five years for the Balfour Declaration to be enacted. This was done by the Statue of Westminster to which King George V gave Royal Assent on 11 December 1931.

The Statute of Westminster transformed the most developed part of the Empire into the Commonwealth of Nations. George V became separately King of Canada, Australia, New Zealand, South Africa, Newfoundland and the Irish Free State, just as he was of the United Kingdom. The Governor-General of Canada became solely his personal representative without reference to the British Government. His coat of arms for the Dominion of Canada became the Royal Arms of Canada. And so on. This new Commonwealth was what Princess

On 29 November 1934 Princess Elizabeth acted as bridesmaid at the marriage of her Uncle the Duke of Kent to Princess Marina of Greece. The wedding photo at Buckingham Palace. From left, back row: King George V; Princess Nicholas of Greece; The Bride Princess Marina, Duchess of Kent; The Groom Prince George, Duke of Kent; Queen Mary; Prince Nicholas of Greece. From left, front row: Princess Elizabeth and Lady May Cambridge (daughter of Queen Mary's brother the Earl of Athlone, Governor-General of Canada 1940–1946, and his wife Princess Alice).

Elizabeth would reign over, Queen individually of most of its monarchies and Head of the Commonwealth for all the realms and the parts that became republics. Her reign would largely be the story of the transformation of the Empire that remained into full Commonwealth membership. Though the public did not quite grasp the new relationship for some time, the framework of the reign of Queen Elizabeth II had been established.

Before passage of the Statute of Westminster the old state of affairs intervened again. Seeing the future of the Crown lay with the Yorks, the Canadian Government in the second half of 1930 asked to have Princess Elizabeth's father as Governor-General of Canada. Ever since the Princess's great-great-great grandfather Prince

Edward the Duke of Kent had lived among them for nearly ten years at the end of the eighteenth century, Canadians had wanted— and repeatedly asked for—members of the Royal Family to come and reside in Canada's fair domain. Several had done so. This time the desire was frustrated by the British Minister for the Dominions, J.H. Thomas. With Princess Margaret just born, the Duchess of York may have been relieved not to have to move her home again, but it remains one of history's might-have-beens to wonder how events would have unfolded if Princess Elizabeth had been reared at Rideau Hall. One thing is certain: Canadians would have been cheered by the Royal Family's presence as they suffered through the bitter years of the Great Depression.

Although the most famous child in the world, Princess Elizabeth still lived a completely unpublic life. This was to change soon. On 29 November 1934, at eight, she was a bridesmaid for her uncle Prince George the Duke of Kent's wedding to beautiful, exotic Princess Marina of Greece. Her real debut in royal public life only

George V's Jubilee was a great Commonwealth event. Princess Elizabeth made her first appearance on a Canadian stamp for the occasion.

came when she was nine however. By temperament and training she was ready for it. King George V and Queen Mary celebrated the Silver Jubilee of their reign, twenty-five years on the Throne, on 6 May 1935. For this great event Princess Elizabeth took her place as the main representative of the third generation of the Royal Family in the moving festivities.

Frank Salisbury's famous painting shows the Royal Family entering St Paul's Cathedral for the Jubilee Service. Princess Elizabeth is seen in flowered pink hat, pink coat and pink shoes, resting her hand reassuringly on Princess Margaret's shoulder. She looks straight out of the canvas with a frank open face as the procession moves along. In the painting of the scene inside the cathedral, a sight of great splendour and beauty, Princess Elizabeth stands at the bottom left of the canvas near the King with her sister, their diminutive size somehow indicating that they, the only two children to be seen in this exclusively adult gathering, must be important.

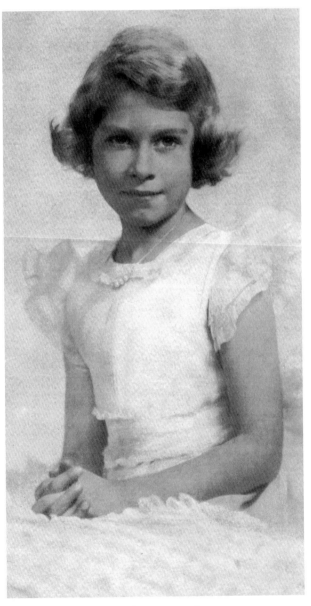

At age 9. Another Marcus Adams portrait photo.

Princess Elizabeth's real debut as a working Princess took place in 1935 when her grandfather's twenty-five years as King was celebrated. She attended the Silver Jubilee service of thanksgiving at St Paul's Cathedral and can be seen in the Salisbury painting of the service.

Afterwards she appeared on the balcony of Buckingham Palace (at Queen Mary's right)

When she joined the King and Queen and the rest of the Royal Family on the balcony of Buckingham Palace afterwards, Princess Elizabeth appeared surprisingly grown up compared with Princess Margaret whose "attempts to raise her chin above the level of the parapet" amused the correspondent of the Canadian *Mail and Empire*.

The Silver Jubilee was a great Commonwealth festival. The Premiers of the Dominions arrived in London for it and took part in the royal procession through the streets. Princess Elizabeth appeared on a special green and white one cent stamp with maple leaves, one of a set of five stamps issued by the Canadian Post Office for the Jubilee which included the King and Queen, Prince of Wales, Duke of York, Windsor Castle and the Royal Yacht *Victoria and Albert III*. Princess Elizabeth had already

been depicted on a Newfoundland stamp some years earlier.

The Princess's next official public appearance was barely a year later. It was a sad one. On 28 January 1936 she watched as her grandfather's coffin was lowered into the grave at Windsor. George V had not long survived his

Some of the races of the Commonwealth depicted in the Silver Jubilee window at St James' Cathedral, Toronto.

Jubilee. Elizabeth had dearly loved the grandfather who terrified the rest of the Royal Family.
And it had been a mutual affection. The old
King had even been seen down on his hands and
knees on the floor allowing Princess Elizabeth to
pull him along by the beard. Every morning
after breakfast the Princess would go to the
window of 145 Piccadilly which could be seen
from Buckingham Palace. At the Palace the
King, binoculars trained on 145, would wave
to her. Before the funeral Elizabeth went to
the lying-in-state of the King when her father
and his brothers held the Vigil of the Princes,
taking their turn standing on guard by their
father's coffin. She felt the loss of her grandfather deeply—in the way of children who soon
recover of course—and grooming her toy horses
at home paused and asked "Oh, Crawfie…ought
we to play?"

Her uncle David was now King Edward VIII
and Princess Elizabeth was second in line to the
Throne. Her parents tried not to let the change
alter her routine. But Elizabeth sensed that
everything was not right. Uncle David no longer
came to tea for one of their riotous card games
as he used to. She did not know it but her parents had been excluded from the new King's
private circle. The King's circle and the Yorks'
represented completely different ways of life.
Edward VIII believed the pleasure he took in
society and the night club and cocktail party cir-
cuit put him on the side of the younger generation of his subjects but in reality the young
people were more attracted by the family life at
Royal Lodge.

Long before his death George V knew about
his son the Prince of Wales' affair with the
American adventuress and divorcee Wallis

Queen Mary's belief in the Crown and her rigid sense of duty were important influ-ences on Princess Elizabeth. Pane of the Silver Jubilee window depicting Her Majesty at St James' Cathedral, Toronto.

Simpson, then the wife of London businessman
Ernest Simpson. "After I am gone, the boy will
ruin himself within six months" George V had
predicted of his son to the British Prime Minister, Stanley Baldwin, in Jubilee Year. To a friend
he said he now hoped the Prince of Wales
would not marry and have a family, adding
"I pray to God that nothing will come between
Bertie and Lilibet and the Throne". On one
occasion the Prince brought the notorious Mrs
Simpson to the Yorks for tea. Tension must
have been in the air for, when they left, Princess
Elizabeth said "Who *is* she, Crawfie?"

A crisis, personal, family and constitutional
shaped up. Edward VIII determined to marry
Wallis Simpson, who was now divorcing Mr
Simpson, regardless of the consequences. He
found the United Kingdom government led by
Stanley Baldwin adamantly opposed. As the
King was Monarch separately of Canada and
the other Dominions his governments there had
to be consulted too. Instead of exercising his
right to consult them directly, Edward VIII, as

Elizabeth's favourite uncle, the still popular Prince of Wales, held the key to her future. He was the Heir to the Throne. If he ever married and had children she would be unlikely to inherit the Crown. The fashionable Prince had quite different ideas about duty than those held by his mother Queen Mary. A section of the Silver Jubilee window at St. James' Cathedral, Toronto, showing the Prince with the Royal Arms of Canada below.

neglectful of his royal prerogatives as of his royal duties, allowed Baldwin to do this for him. Opposition in the Dominions to such a marriage however was even more implacable than in the United Kingdom. Canadians hated the idea of having an American as their Queen. And thanks to the American newspapers which were filled with news of the King's affair, Canadians were better informed about events than the King's subjects in the United Kingdom, where the press had only just broken its silence on the affair.

Her parents said nothing about the crisis but Princess Elizabeth picked up enough of what was going on to be confused by it. She was overheard explaining the situation to her sister. "I think Uncle David wants to marry Mrs Baldwin and Mr Baldwin doesn't like it" she said. The crisis peaked. From their upstairs nursery, Princess Elizabeth and Princess Margaret heard numerous people arriving at the house and leav-

ing. The Duke of York was faced with the prospect of inheriting the Crown and all his personal misgivings about himself returned. To make it worse his main support, the Duchess, came down with severe influenza and was confined to bed. Looking worn and tired, the Duke, in the final days of the crisis, passed from meetings and unpleasant scenes with the King to disagreeable conferences with lawyers. He begged his brother to reconsider. "I've never seen a state paper" he told Lord Louis Mountbatten in despair. But only once did he give way and that was after his last session with his brother when he went to see Queen Mary and "broke down and sobbed like a child".

King Edward VIII signed the instrument of Abdication at 1:52 p.m. on Thursday, 10 December 1936. Princess Elizabeth heard the noise of people gathering in the street outside 145 Piccadilly. There was cheering. She went downstairs and asked a footman what was going on. He told her that the King was abdicating and the Duke of York would be succeeding him. The Princess ran back upstairs and told her sister. Princess Margaret asked Elizabeth if that meant she, Elizabeth, would one day become Queen. "Yes, some day" her sister replied. Crawfie was summoned by the still sick Duchess and told what had happened. According to the governess's account, when their father returned from his proclamation as King George VI on 12 December, Princess Elizabeth and her sister made him a formal curtsey. "He stood for a moment touched and taken aback. Then he stooped and kissed them both warmly." At ten Princess Elizabeth had become the daughter of a King and Heir Presumptive to the Throne.

3

"Ich Dien"

1937–1951

"Ich Dien—I Serve" is the motto of the Heir Apparent to the Throne. As the elder daughter of the new King George VI, Princess Elizabeth would never be officially the Heir Apparent. It was always possible that the King and Queen might have a son, who would take precedence over an elder sister. Princess Elizabeth, for over fifteen years, would remain the Heir Presumptive and, as such, the motto was not hers by right.

But the reality was that the likelihood of a brother was remote at best. The King was 41, the Queen 36. They were not looking to expand their family of two daughters. It was understood by all that Princess Elizabeth would succeed her father in the fullness of time.

Coronation picture of King George VI, Queen Elizabeth, Princess Elizabeth and Princess Margaret. With her father's accession Elizabeth had become Heir Presumptive and her life changed.

Princess Elizabeth was ten years old when her father became King. She would become Queen at the age of 25. The fullness of time was in fact to be these short fifteen years. And, official or not, "I Serve" were the words that would define her perspective on life.

The reign of any monarch is framed by sadness, as the reign begins and ends in death. It starts with the death of the predecessor and ends with the death of the incumbent. For the heir to a throne it is the same. Elizabeth II's years as heir began with the death of her beloved grandfather, King George V, coupled with the abdication and estrangement eleven months later of her closest uncle, King Edward VIII, which brought her father to the Throne. It was, in a sense, a double death that began her years as heir. They would end with the death of a father who doted on her.

But if the beginning and ending were sad in the inevitable way for the Royal Family, the duration of Princess Elizabeth's years as heir were tragic in a larger sense. Most of the world, including the United Kingdom and Canada, was mired in the Great Depression in 1936. The Depression would only end when war came. From 1939 to 1945 her father's realms were then engaged in a life and death struggle with the unspeakable evil of Nazism. After six long years of bombings and fighting and death by the millions, the few years of peace that followed were years of austerity in Britain. People tried to reconstruct their lives amid deprivation and rubble.

Then, like another head of the mythical Hydra, the evil empire of Communism thrived, while its evil twin of Nazism died, and it brought down, in Churchill's memorable phrase, an "Iron Curtain" in Europe. The "Cold War" frosted the international scene. And, as the British Empire began its inexorable decline, starting in Asia, in 1950 another "hot" war began in Korea with the new evil threat. It would cloud the year-and-a-half before Elizabeth II's accession.

These were the years that provided the environment in which a princess grew to become a queen.

Elizabeth II has always had a profound religious underpinning to her life, ignoring the fallacy that modern political theorists present— that in a country, Commonwealth or world of religious diversity, religious tolerance means religion must only be practised in one's private life. One of the most truly tolerant world figures, Queen Elizabeth II has always publicly acknowledged the role of faith in guiding her actions.

The first great event the then Princess Elizabeth, Heir to the Throne, was to participate in was, appropriately therefore, one when Church and State meet for mutual support and strength —the Coronation of her father the King.

Princess Elizabeth was up early the day of the Coronation, awakening at 5:00 a.m. full of energy. She had studied the Coronation service and its significance was in no way lost on her. And she appreciated the beauty of the event. In keeping with the practice of the now King and Queen, from the time when they were Duke and Duchess of York, the two princesses were dressed the same for the ceremony. The only difference was that Princess Elizabeth's train was longer than that of Princess Margaret.

The Royal Family wave to their subjects from the balcony of Buckingham Palace on Coronation Day. It is a scene that is repeated many times in the life of the Commonwealth.

The Coronation was also the first event at which the Princess played a central, albeit subordinate role, in which Canadians took part. The Royal Canadian Mounted Police came for the ceremony. Some British officials wondered if the bearskin headdresses of the guardsmen might not frighten the horses? "Tell them not to worry", the Canadians replied, "We feed the horses bearskins for breakfast every morning". The change in the Crown's role in the Commonwealth that was to dominate her reign had already begun. A new role had evolved for Canada and the other dominions at the Coronation since the Statute of Westminster of 1931 had established their equality with the United Kingdom. The King's Banner for each country was carried in the procession and Princess Elizabeth heard her father crowned as King of Canada, as each realm was named specifically in the Coronation Oath. The Queen would be crowned the same way at her coronation in 1953, by which time she would have also assumed the official title of Queen of Canada. The status of the Princess as Heir to the Throne in 1937 was also recognised around the Commonwealth in the manner in which they celebrated the Coronation. Places such as Princess Elizabeth Land in Australia were named after her, and in Newfoundland Princess Elizabeth's face appeared on a six-cent stamp.

When King George VI and his family moved from their relatively modest home at 145 Piccadilly Street to Buckingham Palace it was a significant moment in Elizabeth's life. The Palace has been her London home ever since—over sixty years—except for a couple of years after her marriage when she resided at Clarence House. And Windsor Castle became and has remained her country house, and true home, when she moved there from Royal Lodge.

The King introduced changes to his elder daughter's academic regime and saw to it that she was interested in statecraft, and trained for her future role as Queen, ensuring that her education was broader than his had been. The King arranged for her to be tutored by Sir Henry Marten, Provost of Eton College, an authority on British constitutional history. Elizabeth Longford described him as a "learned character with just the requisite degree of eccentricity". He kept lumps of sugar in his pocket which he munched, never looked at Princess Elizabeth directly and occasionally addressed her as "gentlemen" as if he were addressing the boys at Eton. The Princess greatly respected him and from him acquired a new enthusiasm for history. She learned to love and admire Queen Victoria and understand how the Queen had influenced policy in a constitutionally correct way.

Queen Mary expanded her practice of taking Princess Elizabeth and Princess Margaret on cultural tours of London to

A Girl Guide company was established at Buckingham Palace to provide the princesses more contact with other children.

The King referred to the immediate Royal Family as "us four". An informal photo in 1939 by Marcus Adam.

The King and Queen discuss their impending trip to Canada with Princess Elizabeth and Princess Margaret, tracing the route on a map.

Formal photograph of Princess Elizabeth in 1939.

various museums. It was also arranged that the princesses would mingle with other children. A girl guide company of thirty-four children was established at Buckingham Palace, for example, including a social mix of daughters of palace staff and chauffeurs as well as members of the household.

In the spring of 1939 the King and Queen travelled to Canada, the first reigning monarchs to tour the Dominion of the North, in what became a memorable royal spring in Canadian history. Canadians had wished for the two princesses to accompany the royal couple but this was not possible. The Queen considered them too young for such a trip. But they were very much on the minds of Canadians that spring. In the messages of loyalty presented to the King, in presents entrusted to their royal

First day cover of Royal Tour with Princess Elizabeth and Princess Margaret depicted on Canadian postage stamp commemorating the tour.

parents, and in the wishes that on the next trip to Canada by the King he would bring them. One of the Canadian postage stamps commemorating the tour included pictures of the two young princesses.

Within the Royal Family the ocean did not provide a barrier either. The princesses had studied their parents' travel plans before the trip and followed their progress during it. With twentieth century technology it was possible for the King and Queen to telephone their daughters from Canada, an opportunity which they took full advantage of.

On her 1951 tour of the Dominion Princess Elizabeth would recall her parents' trip with fondness: "I have always cherished a dream of coming to Canada and ever since the King and Queen came back twelve years ago with tales of its splendours, the dream has been the more compelling."

Princess Elizabeth was thirteen years old when war came to the world in September

VE-Day in London. The King, Queen, Princess Elizabeth and Princess Margaret are joined by Winston Churchill for the traditional balcony appearance.

1939, and nineteen years old when the war ended. VE-Day on, 8 May 1945, celebrated victory in the European campaign, which had ended with Germany's surrender. In the evening, after the Royal Family had appeared on the balcony of Buckingham Palace eight times before the ecstatic crowds, the King agreed, with some natural reluctance, to his daughters' request to join the people celebrating in the streets. Going incognito, but accompanied by their uncle David Bowes-Lyon and others as escorts, the nineteen-year-old Elizabeth and the fourteen-year-old Margaret joined the happy throngs and good naturedly returned with them to the Palace railing, calling out with everyone else "We want the King! We want the Queen!"

The King wrote in his diary that night, "Poor darlings, they have never had any fun yet". Some historians have latched onto this comment as evidence of the restricted and protected life that had been Princess Elizabeth's experience in her teenage years during the war. This was undoubtedly true given the combination of normal royal restrictions and the added fears and tight security of wartime, with the ever present danger of kidnapping or death. But it was, of course a comment by the King, who was also a protective father, explaining to himself, at a moment of high excitement, why he had let them join the crowds against his own instincts. Princess Elizabeth's war years had in fact elements of fun in them and her greatest concern had been not to have more fun so much as a desire to serve the war effort in a larger way than she felt she had been allowed.

When war came it had been decided that London was too dangerous for the princesses.

Some in Britain thought that they should be moved out of the country altogether and the Canadian government offered to provide refuge in Canada, where the Dutch and Norwegian royal families, among others, and many children of ordinary British families went. The Queen's famous remark put an end to such speculation. "They will not go without me", she said, "I won't leave the King, and he will never go". Instead they were sent first to Birkhall, the Scottish home of the King and Queen before their accession, and, when security measures

The two princesses speak to the young people of the Commonwealth and Empire on the "Children's Hour" radio programme in 1940.

were provided, to Windsor Castle, which remained their home for the rest of the war. Nevertheless over three hundred bombs fell on Windsor Park during the hostilities and an air-raid shelter and military defences were built.

As the war progressed the Princess took a more active role with her mother the Queen in making the rounds of military bases and visiting parts of Britain to see and be seen. On 13 October

1940 she gave her first public broadcast on the BBC's *Children's Hour*, which was heard by millions of children around the Commonwealth and Empire. To these children she said "I feel that I am speaking to friends and companions who have shared with my sister and myself many a happy *Children's Hour*. Thousands of you in this country have had to leave your homes and be separated from your fathers and mothers. My sister Margaret Rose and I feel so much for you, as we all know from experience what it means to be away from those we love most of all.... We know, every one of us, that in the end all will be well. For God will care for us, and give us victory and peace. And when peace comes, remember, it will be for *us*, the children of today, to make the world of tomorrow a better and happier place." Princess Elizabeth gave her first public speech at the Mansion

house three-and-half years later, on 31 May 1944. This was for the National Society for the Prevention of Cruelty to Children.

At the Castle there was also time for Christmas pantomimes which the princesses organised and performed each year beginning in 1941, after having created a nativity play in 1940

Princess Elizabeth accompanied her mother the Queen on tours of Commonwealth forces in Britain during the war. Here they visit Canadian soldiers.

Princess Elizabeth in Victorian costume performed in her 1944 pantomime "Old Mother Red Riding Boots" at Windsor Castle.

called *The Christmas Child*. The pantomimes were *Cinderella, Sleeping Beauty, Aladdin* and *Old Mother Red Riding Boots*, the last title showing how their interest in satire had emerged. During the war years Princess Elizabeth achieved fluency in French from advanced studies with a Belgian tutor, Madame de Bellaigue, and began her interest in horse racing.

Of greater concern to Princess Elizabeth was her desire to serve the war effort in what she considered a more tangible way. Several of her cousins were either in the military forces or performing other war work. When she turned sixteen in April 1942 she registered, like every-

The King ensured that his daughter and heir learned the skills of kingship, Royal Lodge, Windsor in wartime Britain, 1942. Reading government papers brought in the famous "red boxes", seen on the table, would be a daily task for the future Queen as it was for the King.

One of her tasks was to sign the reprieve of a convicted murderer. She remarked: "What makes one do such terrible things. One ought to know. There should be some way to help them. I have so much to learn about people."

The Princess persisted in her quest for military service however. She was given her first honorary appointment as Colonel of the Grenadier Guards, and when she inspected them she was a perfectionist. Eventually in the spring of 1945 she was allowed to join the Auxiliary Transport Service or ATS as a second subaltern. She trained as a driver and mechanic and was proud of her proficiency.

Also, not generally known to the public, but known to her family, during the war years Princess Elizabeth had fallen in love

Princess Elizabeth serving in the Auxiliary Transport Service in World War II.

one else her age, for the wartime youth service scheme, but the King did not agree to her actually performing war work. In 1943 the Regency Act was amended however to allow her to be a counsellor of state (and Queen without a regency if her father should die) at the age of eighteen. She acted as a counsellor in 1944 when the King was in Italy. When it was asked if she should not be named "Princess of Wales"? the King said no, that was reserved solely for the wife of a Prince of Wales , and added in his diary that, in any case, "Her own name is so nice."

Sailors, Soldiers, Aviators and Mounties of the Queen

Command-in-Chief of all naval and military forces of Canada is vested in the Queen and, on her behalf, the police forces of Canada enforce her laws. As a result the Queen has a special relationship with her armed and civil forces.

In 1951 Princess Elizabeth toured the ship's quarters of the cruiser HMCS Ontario, *en route from Sydney, Nova Scotia to St John's, Newfoundland.*

On Dominion Day in 1959 the Queen unveiled the memorial to Commonwealth airmen killed while serving in Canada during World War II.

One of the Queen's Household regiments is the Canadian Grenadier Guards of Montreal. In 1992 she presented them with new colours at Rideau Hall.

The Queen is also Colonel-in-Chief of the Royal 22e Régiment du Canada (Valcartier and Quebec City), the 48th Highlanders of Canada (Toronto) and the Calgary Highlanders.

Air Command's 437 Transport Squadron, based in Trenton, Ontario is responsible for flying Her Majesty and members of the Royal Family to Canada for royal tours.

Maritime Command

Queen's Colour

In 1977 Her Majesty authorised a new Queen's Colour for Maritime Command, featuring her cypher.

When the Princess Patricia's Canadian Light Infantry provided the guard at Buckingham Palace in 1999 the Queen inspected the regimental band.

The Royal Canadian Mounted Police have provided the Sovereign's Escort for Her Majesty whenever she is in the capital of Canada, as in 1990, and often escorts the Queen in other cities in Canada and Britain.

with her third cousin Prince Philip of Greece. Prince Philip's parents, Prince Andrew of Greece and Princess Alice of Battenberg, had been forced into exile with the abolition of the Greek monarchy in 1922. (It was to be restored and abolished several times over the decades.) Princess Alice was herself British-born. Prince Philip therefore grew up on the continent and in Britain and was an officer in the Royal Navy.

While they undoubtedly saw each other at family and royal events in their childhood, Princess Elizabeth first took notice of Prince Philip in the summer of 1939 at Dartmouth, when she accompanied her father on a visit to his old naval school, and where Prince Philip was a midshipman. He had been assigned to escort the two princesses. At the time Princess Elizabeth was thirteen and Prince Philip was eighteen.

Despite the absences and difficulties of wartime, with Prince Philip frequently overseas in combat, the infatuation of the young teenager in 1939 grew into the love of a young woman by 1945. With the war ended, Prince Philip proposed in 1946 and Princess Elizabeth accepted. The King was not ready to give his approval however. While he approved of Prince Philip, he thought the Princess was too young and he had a father's natural reluctance to see his daughter leave his immediate family. There were also political concerns. The Greek monarchy had just been precariously restored, and was facing a communist insurrection. Would the marriage have political implications for the British government? If Prince Philip gave up his Greek title to marry the Princess it might be seen as anticipating the fall of the Greek monarchy. If he did not give it up it might sug-

gest the marriage was arranged to bolster the Greek monarchy. And there was the upcoming royal tour of Southern Africa by the Royal Family which the King wished the Princess to undertake. Marriage would have to wait until after the tour.

The 1947 royal trip to Southern Africa would prove to be a seminal event in the future Queen's life in several ways.

First, of course, on a personal level, the love which Princess Elizabeth shared with Prince Philip easily withstood the separation, and Her Royal Highness returned to London intent on pressing her father to consent to a date for their marriage.

Secondly, it gave the mature Princess the opportunity of undertaking at least one tour

Princess Elizabeth's 21st birthday broadcast from South Africa, when she dedicated her life to service, is often recalled by Her Majesty.

The King and his two daughters walk in Natal National Park. The 1947 African tour introduced Princess Elizabeth to both the potential and the troubles of the Commonwealth.

with her parents, from whom she could learn the "ropes" of a royal task which was to become a frequent and essential part of the new monarchy.

Thirdly, it was on this tour that Princess Elizabeth reached the age of majority and in her twenty-first birthday broadcast to the Commonwealth she defined the life to which she was committing herself and which she has lived up to.

"I declare before you all", she stated "that my whole life, whether it be long or short, shall be devoted to your service and the service of our great imperial Commonwealth to which we all belong. But I shall not have strength to carry out this resolution unless you join in it with me, as I now invite you to do; I know that your support will be unfailingly given. God bless all of you who are willing to share it."

The importance of the speech to the Queen herself has been constantly demonstrated by the number of times she has referred to it at subsequent key moments in her life.

Finally, the African tour was important in another dimension. Africa was to play, and continues to play, a central role in the evolution of the Commonwealth, of which Her Majesty is Head. In 1947 she came face to face with the racial and national issues that would inform and bedevil that evolution. As decolonisation came to Africa, starting in the fifties and ending in the eighties, the Commonwealth leadership changed from a "white club" to the most diverse in the world. (The peoples of the Commonwealth had always been that diverse of course.) Much of the Queen's reign has been devoted to dealing with the challenges and opportunities

provided by this continent. As Head of the Commonwealth, Elizabeth II has considered this a vocation to be dealt with mindful of, but independent of, the advice of any one of her governments.

The Royal Family travelled to Cape Town, South Africa on board the battleship HMS *Vanguard*, arriving on 20 February. The tour included South Africa, Swaziland and Rhodesia (now Zimbabwe). The Royal Family, back through Queen Victoria, has always been "colour-blind". They were appalled by the

An early example of the ceremonial pose that would become famous around the world each year on her official birthday in London—riding side-saddle in uniform. The future Queen takes part in the 1947 Trooping the Colour for the King's Birthday as Colonel of the Grenadier Guards.

Charcoal engagement sketch of Princess Elizabeth and Lt Philip Mountbatten was by a Canadian artist and distributed by George Weston Limited of Canada.

racial attitudes they encountered. For example, the King was prohibited by the South African government from speaking or shaking hands with black veterans when presenting them with medals.

Despite the underlying tensions of Afrikaaner racism and nationalism, the tour was a success and included time for sight-seeing as well as official functions. In Swaziland and Rhodesia, freed from government restraint, the Royal Family were able to mix freely with their black as well as their white subjects.

Soon after the Royal Family's return from South Africa, with the Greek crisis resolved in favour of its monarchy, on 8 June 1947 the engagement of Princess Elizabeth and Lieutenant Philip Mountbatten was announced. Philip Mountbatten was the new persona of Prince Philip. To acquire a permanent commission in the Royal Navy, it was necessary that he be a British subject. To become one he renounced his Greek title and claims and adopted his mother's surname, which itself only dated back to 1917. His grandfather, Prince Louis of Battenberg, followed the practice of the Royal Family who renounced their German names and adopted English ones. Years later it was discovered that Prince Philip had already

Official wedding photograph of the royal couple.

been a British subject, as he was a descendant of the Electress Sophia, mother of King George I. When George I, Elector of Hanover became the British King, the Act of Settlement of 1701 provided that all descendants of his mother, in either the male or the female line, were automatically British Subjects, wherever they were born. But that was not realised in 1947 and it was to be as Lieutenant Mountbatten that Prince Philip married the King's daughter. (In 1957 the Queen restored his princely status when she created him a Prince of the United Kingdom.)

The marriage took place on the grey morning of 20 November 1947. The decorations were modest by royal standards due to post-war austerity but the day was still filled with pomp and ceremony and followed enthusiastically by people throughout the Commonwealth. The Labour Government in Britain did not declare a public holiday however. Britain, including the Royal Family, were still under rationing but one hundred extra ration coupons were allotted for the Princess's trousseau. The King created Philip the Duke of Edinburgh on the morning of the wedding.

The newly married royal couple's London home was a suite in Buckingham Palace and for their country home they

rented Windlesham Moor in Berkshire. Their permanent home in London was to be Clarence House (later it would become better known as the home of the Queen Mother) although they would not move in until 1949. The wedding gift from Canada to the Duke was a suite of

By 1950 the Princess and Duke's own family included Prince Charles and Princess Anne

maple furniture and wall panelling for his study in Clarence House. The gift for the Princess was a mink coat.

In 1948 the young couple made their first visit abroad—to Paris. But of greater significance that year was the birth of their first child, Prince Charles, almost exactly a year after their marriage—on 14 November. For the first time in over three hundred years the Home Secretary (or his equivalent in earlier governments) was not present for the birth as it was decided there was no longer a fear that a substitute child would be smuggled into the room. On 15 August 1950 a second child was born to the royal couple, Princess Anne.

The royal couple's stay in Clarence House was, in fact, to be very brief. At Christmas 1949 they moved to Malta where the Duke, still a serving naval officer, had been assigned, and they lived there until the summer of 1951. This was followed by the month long tour of Canada in the autumn.

The years from 1947 to 1951 also saw significant changes in the Commonwealth. First India, Pakistan and Ceylon were admitted as self-governing dominions in 1947, with the same status as the older dominions. But Burma and Ireland decided to leave the Commonwealth and became republics. Then in 1949 the Commonwealth governments agreed that India, which also decided to become a republic, could remain in the Commonwealth as such. While Canada, Australia, New Zealand and the other dominions would remain monarchies with the King as sovereign separately in each country, his old imperial role as the common link between Commonwealth countries—a shared monarchy as well as a shared monarch—was changed to a newly defined role as Head of the Commonwealth and a "symbol" of a more nebulous Commonwealth unity. This was the role that Princess Elizabeth would inherit.

Canada claims, with some justification, to be a maker of monarchs. King George VI and Queen Elizabeth acknowledged this after the 1939 tour of Canada when they explicitly said that it had "made them". But King Edward VII's 1860 tour of Canada as Prince of Wales also was a major element in giving the future king the self-confidence that he was denied by his

Souvenir tablecloth welcoming Princess Elizabeth and the Duke of Edinburgh for their 1951 tour of the Dominion.

mother Queen Victoria. The 1901 and 1908 trips to Canada by the future King George V (as Duke of Cornwall and York and Prince of Wales respectively), were important in his development, if not so critical as his father's 1860 or his son's 1939 trips.

Even Queen Victoria's father, Prince Edward, Duke of Kent, the ancestor of not only the Canadian Royal Family but most of the royal families of Europe, spent nine years—a third of his adult life—and grew to maturity in Canada from 1791 to 1800.

When Princess Elizabeth, accompanied by the Duke of Edinburgh, began her first tour of Canada in October 1951, her first independent tour in the Commonwealth, she was following a familiar path for her family. It was also undertaken with the awareness that it was a dress rehearsal, if one likes, for her future as the Queen. That that future could arrive at any moment was underlined by the fact that Princess Elizabeth travelled with a draft accession declaration in case her father the King, whose health was rapidly deteriorating, should die while the Princess was in Canada.

The tour had been postponed by a week due to the King's September operation for lung cancer, and there was fear that it would not take place at all, but the King was seen to be recovering and the trip was back on. However, due to the lost time the Princess and the Duke of Edinburgh would not sail to Quebec as originally scheduled but would fly to Dorval airport in Montreal and

Princess Elizabeth steps on the soil of her future realm of Canada for the first time on 8 October 1951

then travel back to Quebec where the original arrangements would begin. As a result the Princess and Duke became the first members of the Royal Family to fly the Atlantic, arriving in Montreal on the B.O.A.C. Stratocruiser

Hilton Hassel's famous painting of the Princess and Duke square-dancing at Rideau Hall.

Canopus the morning of 8 October, Thanksgiving day in Canada. The Canadian Post Office issued a special four-cent stamp to commemorate the tour.

The royal couple were greeted by the Governor-General, Viscount Alexander of Tunis and the Prime Minister, Rt. Hon. Louis St-Laurent. Viscount Alexander had commanded the Canadian troops in Italy during World War II and would be leaving office at the end of the year, to be succeeded by Vincent Massey, the first Canadian-born Governor-General since the French regime. The royal train which was to take the Princess and Duke to Quebec, and then across the country, was decorated this day with ears of wheat on the special rear platform to celebrate Thanksgiving. Soon after boarding the train the Princess telephoned her mother the Queen to inquire about her father's health. It was the first day that the Palace had not issued a medical bulletin after the operation, as the King's health seemed to improve. On the day that the Canadian tour started it was also announced that the Princess and the Duke would travel to Africa, Australia and New Zealand in February of the next year.

"Toronto changed the tempo of the tour." The royal couple drive through the streets of Ontario's capital city.

was a feeling of being not far from home.

"Here in Canada, from the welcome you have given me...you have made me feel very much at home..."

In Quebec, the ancient capital of Canada, the Princess retraced the steps of several generations of her family, beginning with her ancestor Prince Edward, Duke of Kent, who had lived there in the 1790s. It was the Duke who first gave voice to the common name of "Canadian" for all British North

The Canadian tour began the future Queen's sense of Canadianism. As her biographer, Elizabeth Longford, quoted one of her staff as noting in later years, "She *feels* Canadian as well as being Queen of Canada, partly because she has been all over it." In 1951 Princess Elizabeth told her future subjects:

"I feel I do not come among you as a complete stranger, for I have met and talked to many Canadians in England, not a few of them in the three services who had come to Europe during the war, and they have told me many things about their homeland.

"I also feel I have addressed a Canadian audience before when on my twenty-first birthday I spoke from Cape Town to all the people of the Commonwealth and Empire.

"Then, I said it was the great privilege of belonging to my family's place in the worldwide Commonwealth that wherever we went there

Receiving a bouquet of flowers from a young ballerina of the Winnipeg Ballet Company. It was to be the first company granted royal patronage by the new Queen in 1952, when she made it the Royal Winnipeg Ballet.

At a specially arranged performance of the Calgary Stampede the
royal couple enjoyed the show,
warmed by a thick blanket in the
freezing temperature of an early
winter day in the Canadian West.

Americans. He broke up a riot in Quebec with the words "Part then in peace. Let me hear no more of the odious distinction of English and French. You are all His Britannic Majesty's beloved Canadian subjects". The Duke was also one of the first advocates of Confederation, urging the union of the provinces nearly a half-century before it was realised. A popular figure with both linguistic communities, he left his name in Quebec on Kent Gate and his legacy in the cheers of "Vive la Princesse" which greeted his great-great-great-granddaughter as she toured the streets of the old town where he had once walked.

From Quebec the royal couple began a thirty-five day tour back and forth across the continent. In Ottawa they placed a wreath at the National War Memorial which her father

had inaugurated, and presented Queen Mary's Carpet to the National Gallery. The *gros-point* needlework carpet had been made by the Princess's grandmother as a wartime fund raiser. It was purchased by the IODE, which in turn gave it to the Princess to present to the Gallery. While in Ottawa the royal couple also took part in various ceremonies, toured the House of Commons, and attended a state dinner at Rideau Hall. On this occasion the Princess and Duke took part in a square dance, properly attired in Canadian country dress of a checked blouse and swinging skirt and checked shirt and blue jeans respectively.

From Ottawa the train took them to Corn-wall, Kingston and Trenton in eastern Ontario. From the Royal Canadian Air Force Station in Trenton they then flew to Toronto, while the

Departing the city hall in Vancouver.

train continued at its own pace to meet them in the capital of Ontario.

Stanley Devon, the only British cameraman on the tour, recounted the arrival in Toronto: "I can claim to have seen every big royal occasion in Britain since 1930. I have seen King Leopold at the height of his popularity in Brussels, the wedding of Princess Juliana at The Hague, and the return of the late King George of the Hellenes to Greece. I even saw Goering and the German troops re-enter an hysterical Rhineland to complete the first of Hitler's coups. None of these had anything on the entry of Princess Elizabeth and the Duke into Toronto. It was dusk when they landed at the airport. It was dark during the seventeen-mile drive to the city centre. But the crowds were denser than in London on V.E.-Day… It continued all next day when they drove for thirty-four miles through the main streets of Toronto…. Toronto changed the tempo of the tour. It set a standard for the rest of Canada to follow, if it could."

The next day they viewed Niagara Falls and in Hamilton it seemed as if the whole city had turned out to welcome them at Civic Stadium, and the tour continued to the same acclaim through southwestern Ontario. In Windsor, the automobile capital of Canada, a toy electric car was given to the royal couple by the Ford Motor company for Prince Charles.

Throughout the country the Princess and Duke saw Canadians of many backgrounds, at

In New Brunswick, the Loyalist Province, the Princess and Duke were presented with a pair of travelling blankets, woven locally and embellished with the royal arms of the province.

Agathe, in the Laurentians of Quebec, where they went sleighing in the snow Canada is famous for, and made a snowman named "Mr Churchill".

Princess Elizabeth ended her trip with remarks that reiterated and reinforced those feelings she had expressed when she started the tour: "In almost every mile that we have travelled through fields, forests, prairies and mountains we have been welcomed with a warmth of heart that had made us feel how truly we belong to Canada…. From the moment when I first set foot on Canadian soil the feeling of strangeness went, for I knew myself to be not only amongst friends, but amongst fellow countrymen."

During the tour the royal couple went to the United States—to Washington and to Arlington, to meet the current American President Harry Truman and to pay tribute to the Americans' first president, George Washington (Elizabeth is one of the closest living relatives of George Washington) at Mount Vernon. Mr Truman

work, at play and at their places of worship. There were longer stops in the major cities and towns, and a number of ten-minute stops in smaller communities. They saw factories, shipping, grain elevators, and natural resources industries. There were military reviews, religious services, unveilings and banquets, ceremonial drives and massive gatherings. There was a football game between Edmonton and Winnipeg, a hockey game in Montreal, a lacrosse match in Vancouver and the Calgary Stampede.

In short, to the extent that it was possible in a month, they saw Canada and became a part of Canada. The early arrival of winter even allowed time for a "winter holiday" toward the end of the trip in a chalet in Ste

In a countryside blanketed by an early snowfall, the royal couple leave church in St Agathe, Quebec.

greeted her as "a Canadian Princess" and the reception for the eight Commonwealth ambassadors in Washington was held by the Princess at the Canadian Embassy.

Canada and the United States had once been enemies, Canadians fighting their American neighbours on several occasions in the eighteenth and nineteenth centuries to preserve their royal identity. In the twentieth century they had become friends and the Princess noted that "Here [in North America] the most spacious monarchy and the most powerful republic dwell side by side in easy friendship."

At the traditional luncheon at the London Guildhall on 19 November, following the royal tour of Canada, the Princess spoke about her experience. She said that "[Canadians] have placed in our hearts a love … which will never grow cold and which will always draw us back again."

King George VI had the satisfaction of knowing that his daughter and heir had received from Canadians the same warm and loyal affection that he and Queen Elizabeth had twelve years before in 1939. Demonstrating his pride in a tangible way he created both Princess Elizabeth and the Duke of Edinburgh members of the Most Honourable Privy Council in recognition of their successful tour. On 31 January 1952 Princess Elizabeth and the Duke left for a tour of Africa and Australasia. This tour had been scheduled for the King and Queen but the King's illness and operation had resulted in it first being postponed and then transferred to Elizabeth and Philip to undertake. The royal couple were seen off at the airport by the King. It was the last time Princess Elizabeth would see her father, and the tour would be cut short.

The Princess and the Duke arrived in Kenya,

"A Canadian Princess" in Harry Truman's words, Princess Elizabeth entertains the American President as hostess in the Canadian Embassy in Washington.

and by 5 February they were staying at Treetops Hotel. It was a resthouse, with three bedrooms, a dining room, a small room for the hunter/guard and a platform for viewing wildlife. It was literally a treehouse—built into the branches of a giant thirty-foot wild fig or *mgumu* tree. Below was a salt-lick and pool visited nightly by rhino, warthogs and other wild animals. The next morning, 6 February 1952, while the royal couple slept at Treetops, King George VI died in his sleep in England. Later in the day Princess Elizabeth learned that she had in fact awoken that morning as Queen Elizabeth II. That she learned this not in England, but in one of her African lands, en route to her Pacific realms, and only months after returning from her Canadian kingdom, illustrated the future that awaited her.

IMAGES OF MAJESTY

Paintings, statues, plaster reliefs, bronzes, stamps and drawings have been among the many media used to convey the Queen's image throughout her reign.

A 1950's portrait of the Queen by James Gunn depicted Her Majesty in the stately tradition. One of several copies of the portrait is in the Saskatchewan Legislature.

The painting of the Queen in the robes of the Order of St John, by Leonard Boden, was the one chosen by the Alberta Legislature to hang in its building.

Another painting of the Queen in a more modern style hangs in the Queen Elizabeth Theatre at the Canadian National Exhibition grounds in Toronto.

An image of the Queen as the Canadian "Statue of Liberty".

In 1962 Sir Charles Wheeler, President of the Royal Academy created these three bronze busts of Her Majesty.

The relief cast used for the first design of the obverse of Canadian coins by a Canadian artist—Dora de Pedery-Hunt. It shows Her Majesty wearing the state diadem.

A statue of the Queen graces the grounds of the Manitoba Museum of Man and Nature in Winnipeg,

A relief image of the Queen by Toronto artist Jaroslav Huta was presented to Her Majesty by the Canadian Government. It was also used as the basis for the definitive stamp of the Queen issued by Canada Post in the 1980's.

The 1960's series of definitive stamps in various denominations showed an image of the Queen with scenes from Canadian life in the background.

The statue of the Her Majesty unveiled on Parliament Hill in 1992. It was created by Jack Harman and depicts the Queen riding astride not side-saddle as she was always seen at Trooping the Colour ceremonies.

The Queen on a Moose —The well-known Canadian artist Charles Pachter's famous painting of Elizabeth II as a Canadian icon.

4

"By the Grace of God...Queen"

Canadian Royal Style & Title, 1953

1952–1954

Elizabeth II, born in a plain London town house, came to the Throne in a place seemingly even more unlikely. She was still at Treetops Hotel, a wildlife observation resthouse, among the people of her African province of Kenya, on 6 February 1952 when her father's death was reported. The arrival of the news itself was irregular. A reporter, not an official, first got through by telephone to her Private Secretary, Martin Charteris, with the unconfirmed rumour that the King was dead. In fact that historic day was normal in just one way. As in any family, it was the new Queen's husband, the Duke of Edinburgh who broke the sad news to her "as she stood in a white dress under an over clouding sky".

Treetops Hotel, Kenya, where Princess Elizabeth became Queen Elizabeth II.

Arrival of the new Queen in London awaited by her United Kingdom Cabinet.

vious year was finally opened. Asked by her Private Secretary what her regnal name would be, the Queen said "My own, of course—what else?" And Queen Elizabeth II signed her first state paper as Monarch.

She arrived back in London on 7 February. Dressed all in black the young Queen came down the steps from her plane alone, awaited on the tarmac by her United Kingdom Prime Minister and Cabinet. That is the poignant scene that will forever evoke the start of her reign. It is as deeply imprinted on history as the picture of her ancestor Victoria receiving the Archbishop of Canterbury and Lord Conyngham at Kensington Palace when they came to tell her she was Queen.

Among those present in London at this moment was Vincent Massey the new Canadian Governor-General. One of the final acts of King George VI had been to appoint the first Canadian born person in modern times to represent the King in Canada. Massey was a Privy Counsellor and in that capacity attended the Queen's first Council at St James's Palace the next day. In his memoirs, *What's Past is Prologue*, written years later, he recalled how

For a moment confusion prevailed among the royal entourage thus taken by surprise. Telegrams had to be sent, the 4,000 mile flight back to London arranged, mourning clothes obtained from the ship that was to have conveyed the royal couple to Australasia. Overwhelmed as she was by grief for the dearly loved father with whom she had had such a close relationship, Elizabeth nonetheless quietly attended to everything necessary. The envelope with the draft Accession Declaration that had gone across Canada and back with her the pre-

the Queen, a slight figure dressed in mourning, entered the great room alone, with strong but perfectly controlled emotion, went through the exacting tasks the Constitution prescribes. Her speeches were perfectly delivered. After this, Prince Philip, who was in the room as a Privy Councillor, stepped forward quietly and went out the door with her.

The sight of this "fair and youthful figure"—as Churchill called her—grieving but intent on duty, touched countless hearts. A woman at the top was still, midway through the twentieth century, an anomaly. For centuries monarchy had been almost the only way a woman ever could achieve such a status, and even so, there were difficulties. Matilda, the first female to inherit the Throne, was driven from it by her rough barons. Not till Mary I in 1552 was the first Queen regnant enthroned. Even the fiery Elizabeth I herself found occasion to reprimand her—exclusively male—advisors for talking to her in a way they would not have used had she "been crested not cloven". So it was fitting that the second half of the century, the era when the condition of women was to be so radically altered, should begin with the accession of a great Queen, a Queen as hard working and professional as any man.

Elizabeth II can have felt only relief when, after the lying in state and other funeral rites—which provided the other unforgettable vignette of the Accession—the three Queens, Elizabeth II, Elizabeth and Mary veiled in black, mourning father, husband and son—her father was buried at Windsor on 14 February. The glare of public attention was sufficiently diminished for the Sovereign to get on with being Queen. And so she began a lifetime routine: the perpetual red (and other colour) boxes crammed with state papers, weekly audiences with her United Kingdom Prime Minister, reception of diplomats, foreign sovereigns and visiting heads of state, administrative matters and visits, tours and receptions for her other realms. Her first visit to the old Scottish capital of Edinburgh was successfully made in July. In November came

The grieving Queen reaches Clarence House.

her first Remembrance Sunday and her first opening of a session of Parliament.

Those who dealt with the new Sovereign were impressed with her concentration, efficiency, and thoroughness. She was punctual and self-disciplined. Somehow they had not expected it. And she also had courage. At first she felt timid about receiving the Prime Minister, but soon he and the other ministers were the ones on edge, realising that if they failed to read all the state papers in advance, they were in danger of being caught out by their Queen who did. Elizabeth II was also found to be decisive and possessed of common sense.

The Queen's Royal Style and Title, enacted by her Canadian Parliament in 1953, is used on commissions, letters patent and other official documents such as Her Majesty's proclamation of the Maple Leaf Flag in 1965.

The first big state event facing the Queen was her Coronation. She appointed the Duke of Edinburgh as chairman of the commission entrusted with the demanding job of planning and organising the massive one-day celebration. It was April 1952 when the Coronation Commission's first meeting was held, more than a year before the event itself. Cost was a major factor in its deliberations. The crowning would be expensive, four million dollars in fact. But to the government and planners it was justified. The celebration would provide a happy respite in an economically bleak world, a world emerging slowly from post-war austerity only to find itself in a cold war and arms race. Also the cost

of the Coronation was moderate compared with the fifty million dollar bill for the 1952–1953 election and inauguration of the American President, Dwight Eisenhower.

Elizabeth II had, of course, been proclaimed at Ottawa too on 6 February 1952. Canada being between Governors-General, the task fell to the Chief Justice, Thibeaudeau Rinfret, who was acting as Administrator of the Government. "The High and Mighty Princess Elizabeth Alexandra Mary" the Canadian proclamation declared, was "Queen" and "Supreme Liege Lady in and over Canada". The Queen's actual title was not agreed on until the Commonwealth Prime Ministers' Conference in London in December. It was then decided that she would have separate titles in each of her realms but they would be inserted into a common formula. For the first time too the Monarch would have the title "Head of the Commonwealth". The Parliaments of the different realms then got busy providing legal embodiment for the change. The Canadian Parliament did so on the eve of the Coronation.

Adoption of the separate title "Queen of Canada" for Elizabeth II was more than further recognition of national independence. It was the fulfilment of a dream. Without the Crown there would never have been a Canada; the country would have become part of the United States.

At Confederation in 1867, Canadians wanted the newly united provinces called "The Kingdom of Canada". Though they pressed for this right up to the final draft, they were denied their legitimate aspiration when American hostility to the union made itself felt in London. Only then did the Fathers of Confederation come up with the term "Dominion" as a monarchical equivalent to kingdom that the Americans were less likely to find offensive.

The preamble to the British North America Act 1867 (now called the Constitution Act 1867) referred loftily to how uniting the provinces would "promote the interests of the British Empire". But the chief architect of

Queen Victoria receiving Sir John A. Macdonald on the eve of Confederation 1867. Elizabeth II's title "Queen of Canada" was the fulfilment of Macdonald's dream of The Kingdom of Canada.

Confederation, the Prime Minister Sir John A. Macdonald, who was the firmest believer in the vision of "The Kingdom of Canada", was even then looking beyond empire to a day when the new Canada might be on its own. At least that is what his famous words to Queen Victoria appear to mean.

On the eve of Confederation, following the London Conference and when the Confederation legislation was making its way through the Parliament of Westminster, Queen Victoria received Macdonald in audience at Buckingham Palace. It was 27 February 1867 and the Queen was attended by her daughter Princess Louise. When Her Majesty congratulated her Canadian Prime Minister on the success of his measure, Macdonald replied that the purpose of Confederation was "to declare in the most solemn and emphatic manner our resolve to be under the Sovereignty of Your Majesty and your family forever".

Here was no mention of the British Empire but only the basic relationship of monarchy—the bond between Sovereign and Canadian people. Canada down the road might become completely independent, perhaps a greater country than the United Kingdom. But even in that case Macdonald wanted it to be endowed with the institutions of hereditary, parliamentary monarchy and the descendants of Queen Victoria. To make this clear to posterity, the old campaigner recorded the words he used at the audience in a letter to his sister.

Balked of his Kingdom of Canada, Macdonald, in the years that followed, kept referring unofficially to Queen Victoria as "Queen of Canada" all the same. It was with Victoria's

great-great-granddaughter that this dream of the Kingdom of the North was now finally and formally achieved when, on 29 May 1953, Elizabeth II's new title was proclaimed. Discussion of the Royal Style and Titles Act in Parliament showed that its history-making character was appreciated.

The Prime Minister and two future Prime Ministers spoke in the Commons on the second reading of the bill on 3 February 1953. It was Lester Pearson, future leader of a Liberal Government in the sixties, who recounted the story of how the framers of Confederation wanted the country recognised as the Kingdom of Canada. Macdonald, Pearson said, "would welcome the introduction of the legislation". He also pointed out how on King Edward VII's Accession in 1901 another Canadian Prime Minister, Sir Wilfrid Laurier, tried unsuccessfully to have "King of Canada" put into the Royal Style and Title. The title "Queen of Canada" for Elizabeth II was important, Pearson said, because monarchy "ensured a more solid and secure foundation for national development than might otherwise be the case under some other form of democratic government". The Crown stood for "peace, dignity and ordered progress".

John Diefenbaker, soon to be the new Progressive Conservative Prime Minister, traced the history of the royal title from the reign of the Saxon King Egbert who a thousand years before called himself "King of the English". This was changed to "Queen of Great Britain" under Queen Anne and in 1901 "of the British Dominions beyond the Seas" had been added for the self-governing Dominions. Diefenbaker pointed out that without the "centralising mystical influence of the Crown" it "would have been impossible to bind together the various races and religions" of the Commonwealth in all parts of the world.

Louis St Laurent, the Prime Minister, gave the House a definition of a shared monarch when he told the members that the new royal style and title recognised

> that our parliament is headed by the sovereign; and that it is the sovereign who is recognised as the sovereign of the United Kingdom who is our sovereign and who is loyally and, I may say, affectionately recognised as the sovereign of our country.

He also explained why the title "Defender of the Faith" was appropriate for Canada. Though Canada had no established churches, many Canadians believed human affairs were directed by an all-wise Providence. It was therefore "a good thing that the civil authorities would proclaim that their organisation is such that it is a defence of the continued belief in a supreme power that orders the affairs of men" and there could be no reasonable objection to having the Queen "the head of the civil authority, described as a believer in and a defender of the faith in a supreme ruler". In short "Defender of the Faith" in Canada meant that the Crown was the defender of religious freedom.

After the third reading of the Royal Style and Title Bill, Mr St Laurent invited the members to stand and sing the Royal Anthem, which they hastened to do.

The Queen's grandmother, Queen Mary,

asked in her will that if she died before the Coronation the ceremony not be postponed or diminished in grandeur because of mourning for her. Her concern was prophetic. The old Queen died on 24 March 1953 thereby missing the crowning of her granddaughter which would have been her fourth Coronation. Elizabeth II could only briefly mourn the formidable grandmother who had so important an influence on her formation and who, as her "old Grannie and subject", had first greeted her as Queen by

Canadian Coronation stamp.

kissing her hand in the time honoured but by then rarely used fashion. The Coronation took place as planned less than three months later on Tuesday 2 June 1953.

No previous monarch was crowned in so intentionally Commonwealth a way. Thousands of people flocked to London from the Dominions. The Canadians occupied whole viewing stands in Parliament Square. Participants in the street procession ranged from red coated Mounties from Canada to bareheaded men of Fiji in scarlet jackets and white skirts, as well as guests

The ceremonial bracelets called Armills were the gift of Canada and the other monarchies of the Commonwealth to the Queen.

like the 6' 3" Queen Salote of Tonga. New bracelets called Armills were added to the royal regalia as a present to the Queen from the Commonwealth governments. At the Queen's own insistence floral emblems of the member countries decorated her gorgeous Coronation dress. The coats of arms of the Commonwealth appeared on the wall of the special Annexe to Westminster Abbey and Canadian troops relieved Australian soldiers in guarding the Palace. A special honour was conferred on Canada's leading composer Healy Willan who was asked to write one of the Anthems for the Homage. The banner of the Royal Arms of Canada was carried by the Canadian High Commissioner in the Abbey procession.

The day itself dawned cold and drizzly. The first of the nine carriage processions reached Westminster Abbey, where 7,500 invited guests waited, at 8:45 a.m. The Queen herself arrived from the Palace at 11:00 in the slow moving eighteenth century Gold State Coach. And the immemorial rite began. As Her Majesty moved up the aisle of the Abbey, scholars from Westminster School shouted out the ancient Latin salute "Vivat Regina!" At the Recognition, where the Monarch is presented to her subjects, the Queen made a graceful curtsey each time the people responded with "God Save Queen Elizabeth". Then she took her oath to her peoples, Canada being mentioned second as her most senior realm after the United Kingdom. The Monarch's oath is a reciprocal one. She makes her pledge to her people and they, when they enter her service, swear an oath of allegiance to her.

Divested of all her robes and jewellery and dressed in a plain white shift, Elizabeth II was anointed with holy oil seated in St Edward's

Knights of the Garter hold a canopy over the Queen for the anointing. The anointing is directly patterned on that of Solomon, King of Israel, nearly 3,000 years ago.

Chair. This part of the rite came directly from the anointing of the Jewish King Solomon of Israel by Zadok the priest and Nathan the prophet nearly three thousand years before. Next the Queen received the outward symbols of majesty and items of regalia—robes, spurs, sword, bracelets—and finally the royal robe and stole, on the former of which Commonwealth emblems shared their place with embroidered eagles deriving from Byzantium and the Roman Empire.

When the orb, ring, sceptre and glove, symbols of the royal dignity, had been presented, the Archbishop placed St Edward's Crown on Elizabeth II's head and all cried "God save the Queen!" Laden with the regalia the Queen was attended from St Edward's Chair to her Throne and symbolically lifted into it. Those who had been touched by the sight of the four-year-old Prince Charles brought in to sit with his grandmother Queen Elizabeth the Queen Mother in the Royal Gallery to see his mother crowned, were now stirred by that of the Queen's young husband the Duke of Edinburgh doing homage to her, pledging to become her "liege man of life and limb", touching her Crown and kissing her on the left cheek.

The Homage completed, the Eucharist continued and the newly crowned Queen and her husband knelt reverently and bare headed together to receive the Blessed Sacrament. During the singing of the Te Deum, having resumed the Crown again, the Queen passed into St Edward's Chapel for the Recess. She emerged wearing the lighter Imperial State Crown and the gold and ermine trimmed purple velvet robe. As she proceeded down the long

Maples leaves and other floral emblems of her realms decorated the Queen's sumptuous Coronation dress.

One of the most moving parts of the Coronation was when the Queen, crowned and enthroned, received the homage of her husband, the Duke of Edinburgh.

members of the Royal Family made six appearances on the balcony for the crowds massed below. At the third appearance, the Queen switched on the lights of the London illuminations and the city came alive. Palace lights were finally dimmed only at midnight but the jubilant crowds danced in the cold streets until 3:00 a.m.

Canada At The Coronation, produced by The Ryerson Press in July 1953, captures this exciting moment in time for the Canadians in Coronation London, civilians and service personnel alike. Hundreds are seen seated on the ballroom floor of Canada House eating lunch picnic style following the ceremony. "Canadian Girls" wearing big rosettes with a picture of the Queen in the centre wave and smile for the camera. In the street outside Ontario House the provincial arms and Canadian Red Ensign are displayed. A group of RCAF pilots taking part in the flypast for the Queen pose for a black and white photo and members of the Canadian contingent pin on their Coronation Medals in unison at a Coronation Investiture held by the Queen at Buckingham Palace.

It is hard today to appreciate the degree to which Elizabeth II's Coronation caught the eye of the world. But catch it it did. Women in Vienna sported Coronation hairdos of stylised crowns. Far away in Korea, the Royal Canadian Artillery and Lord Strathcona's Horse, fighting

aisle of the Abbey everyone joined in singing God Save the Queen, many with tears of emotion in their eyes. After a light lunch in the Annexe the Queen and Duke left at 3:13 p.m. in pouring rain for the two mile procession back to the Palace, a procession of 12,000 armed forces officers and personnel that took forty minutes to pass a single point.

Popular enthusiasm—people had been camped on the street for three days in the inhospitable weather—was not dampened by the downpour. Moving at a stately pace through the bedecked but dripping London, where arches, crowns, flags and bunting bravely hid the grim damage from wartime bombs, the royal procession reached the Palace six-and-a-half hours after setting out in the morning. During the remainder of the day, the Queen and Duke, the Queen Mother, Princess Margaret and other

The famous Cecil Beaton Coronation photograph of Her Majesty wearing the Imperial State Crown, holding the Orb and Sceptre and wearing the Armills and Ring.

Inside Canada House hundreds of Canadians had lunch sitting on the ballroom floor following the Coronation.

opposite Hill 227, marked the day by firing red, white and blue smoke shells at the enemy—the Communist army of North Korea—and the 3rd Battalion of the Royal Canadian Regiment drank their Sovereign's health in a special rum ration. Even in the republican United States it was the same. Innumerable Coronation parties were held. One in New York was attended by the Queen's uncle, ex-King Edward VIII and his wife the Duchess of Windsor who, perhaps unconscious of the irony of doing so, both donned paper crowns at the event. The new Soviet Ambassador to the United Kingdom, Jakov Malik, also sat among the guests in the Abbey witnessing "what his country had perhaps sacrificed when it rejected the evolutionary development of a monarchical society".

Part of the reason for unparalleled world attention was the new medium of television.

Royal Canadian Mounted Police reach the end of the Coronation Procession through the streets of London.

Fearful the fuss of televising with cameras and lights might disrupt the Coronation service, the Queen was at first against allowing it. The United Kingdom Cabinet therefore formally advised her that the Coronation not be televised. But public disappointment at the decision made the Queen realise how much her people wanted to see and be part of her Coronation so she changed her mind and got the Cabinet to reverse its decision. As a result, just seven-and-a-half hours after the end of the service, TV films of the Coronation were on the last lap of their flight to North America, and Canadians were able to watch it in late afternoon or evening of Coronation Day.

Though attention was riveted on London, Coronation Day was a very big day in Canada. Varying the general pattern of celebrations—parades, tattoos, religious services (denominational and inter-denominational) and speeches—were local events illustrating the traditional

cultural diversity of the country. The parade in St John's—Newfoundland had joined Canada only four years before—was the largest in the city's history. Ninety thousand boxes of candy with the Queen's picture on them were given to school children in the province, some dropped by RCAF planes to make sure youngsters in outlying places got them on the day. Horse racing and fireworks marked celebrations in Prince Edward Island, the island province named for the Queen's great-great-great grandfather Prince Edward, Duke of Kent, and at Halifax the royal standard was raised on Citadel Hill where the Duke built the third fortification. In New Brunswick crowds took the oath of allegiance together and on the American border the United States town of Calais closed schools and shops to celebrate jointly with its Canadian twin St Stephen.

"French Canada is unswervingly loyal to the Monarchy" observed Robert Stead in describing festivities in Quebec for his account of Coronation Day for the August *Canadian Geographical Journal.* The main public event in Montreal attracted 400,000 people and at Fletcher's Field the Mayor, Camilien Houde, led 100,000 in marking the day. Cardinal Léger celebrated Pontifical High Mass at St James' Basilica "for divine guidance of the young Queen" and in the capital, Quebec City, celebrations took place on the Plains of Abraham.

At night beacons and bonfires were lit in many parts of Toronto, the Ontario capital, where local ethnic groups staged a gigantic Coronation Show at the Canadian National

The Queen passes Canada House in the Gold State Coach on her return to the Palace.

Exhibition stadium. Seventy civic groups in Hamilton co-ordinated the largest celebration of the steel city's history, the programme including a full scale regatta. Farther west, citizens of Winnipeg heard their Lieutenant-Governor point out that "the people of Manitoba have come from almost every country to make their homes in Canada, but they are united in loyalty and devotion, and join in wishing for our gracious Sovereign a long, peaceful, and happy reign".

Saskatchewan events had been co-ordinated by a provincial committee which contacted 600 communities. Out of this came 125 pooled celebrations and a pageant written and composed by Neil Harris of Saskatoon. Square dancing and "the colourful Elks band from Williston, North Dakota" were also features of the festivities. Alberta was the only province where it rained on Coronation Day, storms forcing some cancellations. At Edmonton ethnic groups in national dress were much in evidence. The postmaster of the tiny community of Coronation, Alberta—named to mark the crowning of George V in 1911 —"was kept busy cancelling thousands of stamps on request of philatelists from almost all parts of the world". And in Victoria the Chinese community staged a lion dance. British Columbia's metropolis, Vancouver, significantly featured "massed TV sets bringing the London telecasts to thousands of viewers".

In Ottawa 100,000 people gathered on Parliament Hill on Coronation Day. To a trumpet fanfare the Royal Standard was broken out. The capital's programme included a parade of 7,000 men and women of the forces, trooping the colour, religious observances and Coronation music. An official version of "God Save the

Coronation Day in Ottawa. Massed Army, Navy and Air Force contingents on Parliament Hill wait for the ceremonies to begin. A silhouette of the Queen decorates the Peace Tower.

Queen" in French was authorised, finally standardising different sets of words in use for a long time. The highlight was the Queen's address which, here as elsewhere across the country, was the focal point of the day's observances.

Elizabeth II was profoundly moved by the experience of the Coronation and the oneness she had felt with her peoples. "The sense of spiritual exaltation that radiated from her was almost tangible to those of us who stood near her in the Abbey" commented Dermot Morrah,

a herald who took part. People noted a new serenity about her afterwards. "Calm in joy, calm in grief" is how the Queen's biographer Lady Longford has expressed it. The Queen herself said "I no longer feel anxious or worried".

This new state was reflected in her Coronation Address to the Commonwealth. In it the Queen made clear what the event signified to her. "I have in sincerity pledged myself to your service, as so many of you are pledged to mine" she said. For her the Coronation was "not the symbol of a power and a splendour that are gone, but a declaration of our hopes for the future". In other words, just as a hockey or football match, a concert or session of court is conducted in a form created years before any of the players or participants were born, so the Monarchy long ago found the form that best expressed its special act of dedication—a coronation. It involved dressing up—as judges, soldiers, scholars or brides do—but for a purpose related more to the present and future than the past.

Vincent Massey, the most intellectual of the Canadian-born Governors-General, understood the philosophical and historical dimensions of the Crown as well as anyone. Following the Queen, he too probed to the heart of the Coronation's meaning in his radio broadcast on the CBC that day. The Coronation meant more than a spectacle he said, "It is part of ourselves. It is linked in a very special way with our national life. It stands for qualities and institutions which mean Canada to every one of us and which for all our differences and all our variety have kept Canada Canadian". Above all the Crown was an enduring, living thing. "The Queen is the head of our nation, and our nation, as we contemplate her Headship, becomes a household itself."

Coronation related activities—such as the great naval review at Spithead in which the Royal Canadian Navy was prominent—continued after 2 June. It was barely five months later on 23 November 1953 that the Queen set out on her first great tour as Queen, an expanded version of the interrupted visit to the Antipodes of the previous year. Canada, not included in the itinerary since the Queen as Princess was there two years before, nevertheless got a tiny share when Her Majesty and the Duke of Edinburgh made a brief refuelling stop at Gander, Newfoundland at 3:23 a.m. the next day. "It's nice to be in Canada again, even if only for a short stay", the Queen told the crowd who despite the cold had been waiting all night. Their boisterous rendering of "She's a jolly good fellow" had woken her and made her decide to get dressed and go out to speak to them.

When public events touch people's drinks they have certainly penetrated their consciousness. A Coronation advertisement.

Robert Lacey in *Majesty* regards the 1953-1954 Commonwealth tour as the long delayed international celebration of victory in the war. Coming so close to the Coronation it appeared to many to be connected with that great ceremony. In fact it was the continuation of the Sovereign's tours of the overseas realms begun in 1939 to show the King's new position as Monarch of each separately. Postponed by World War II, the tours were resumed when George VI went to South Africa in 1947 but then shelved again because of his failing health and death.

It was the greatest tour the Queen would make in fifty years of her reign. It took 173 days and involved 43,618 miles—10,000 by plane, 900 by car, 2,500 by rail and the rest by sea. It was the first great round the world tour of a monarch and began a pattern that would make Elizabeth II the most travelled monarch in history. From Newfoundland the royal stratocruiser *Canopus* flew to Bermuda. The tiny Atlantic island was en fête. "Welcome to our Gracious Queen / Who we have loved but never seen" was the chorus of the calypso inspired by the visit. Locals competed for creating the best decorative arch and the Queen toured each parish and town, addressed the Legislature and—

This Brownie in St Ann's, Jamaica, was not the least disconcerted by the sudden arrival of a stray dog as she was about to present a bouquet. She carried through to the satisfaction of her Queen and the amusement of the Duke of Edinburgh.

motor traffic having only recently been permitted on the island—rode in the smallest car ever used on a royal tour route.

From Bermuda the Queen flew to Jamaica and landed at the holiday resort of Montego

Bay. From there she drove 120 miles through the heart of the 4,413 square mile Caribbean Island, travelling past palm shaded coral beaches and over inland mountains, to reach Kingston the capital. In two days she carried out many functions. After a children's rally at Sabrina Park, Her Majesty planted the first of a "salute of a million trees" to combat erosion and then addressed the Jamaican Legislature. She also held an investiture, visited the new University College of the West Indies and took in historic sites. Before leaving she and the Duke experienced a tropical downpour and enjoyed a swim in the warm ocean.

The royal couple boarded the liner SS *Gothic* for the next phase of their tour. On board there was time—and more important, privacy—for relaxation before the ship reached the Panama Canal Zone on 29 November. The Queen drove the length of the waterway connecting the two great oceans. She experienced a phenomenon that would be repeated many times in years ahead—a fanatically exuberant, and in this case noisily Latin, welcome *from a republic*.

A three week cruise took them to Fiji where chiefs boarded the *Gothic* to present the Queen with a Tambua or whale's tooth, the traditional invitation to land. At Albert Park in Suva, the Fijian capital, Her Majesty drank the traditional coconut drink Kava and watched Fijian dancers. At night she was escorted to the state ball by torchbearers who ran alongside her car making "a line of leaping, moving flame through the city". After a visit to the sugar plantations of Viti Leven worked by the Indian population of Fiji, the royal couple left by flying boat for

With Queen Salote of Tonga on the 1953–54 Commonwealth world tour.

Tonga, the scattered 169 volcanic islands called the Friendly Islands by the explorer Captain Cook.

There to welcome her was the island's Queen Salote who had won the acclaim of London crowds on Coronation Day for refusing, despite the rain, to put up her carriage top and spoil their view of her. Kukualofa, the Tongan capital, gaily decorated for the visit in the languorous Polynesian style, had an enormous carpet of tapa, the fabric of the island, covering the length of the roadway of the processional route. The Queen and Duke stayed at the Royal Palace, a spacious Victorian building with wide verandahs. The Palace grounds ran down to the sea and spotting them were fifty burning watch-fires as Tongan warriors guarded their guests. The Queen attended a great feast which was thrown open to the public after she and Queen Salote retired. "Seldom has so much been eaten by so many who left so little" says Wynford Vaughan Thomas of this banquet in his *Royal Tour 1953-4*. At dawn on Sunday the Queen was serenaded by flutes blown with the nose. Tonga is the world's only Methodist monarchy so the Queen attended the newly built Methodist Church that day. Later she saw the famous tortoise Tui Malila said to have been brought to the islands by Cook.

Then it was on to New Zealand where the Queen and Duke of Edinburgh spent Christmas. It was New Zealand's equivalent of Canada's 1939 tour—the first time the reigning Monarch had come for an extended stay. "Can you wonder that I am proud to be here?" said the Queen thanking the thousands of New Zealanders who turned out to greet her when the *Gothic* reached Auckland, the country's largest city, on 23 December. She broadcast the second Christmas Message of her reign from Government House where she said she was "completely and most happily at home" though, mentioning that "we all want our children at Christmas time", she added poignantly, "I hope perhaps mine are listening to me now and I am sure that when the time comes they, too, will be great travellers" "I set out on this journey" she said "in order to see as much as possible of the people and countries of the Commonwealth and Empire, to learn at first hand something of their triumphs and difficulties and something of their hopes and fears". She also revealed how she saw her own vocation: "I want to show that the Crown is not merely an abstract symbol of our unity but a personal and living bond between you and me".

Besides experiencing Christmas in a warm climate with traditional holiday fare of turkey and plum pudding but with Santa Claus arriv-

Opening her New Zealand Parliament in Wellington.

ing in a carriage drawn by six ponies, the Queen carried out a packed schedule making a thorough tour of her 103,740 square mile realm. The first part of the five-week sojourn was devoted to North Island. At a huge Maori gathering at Waitangi on 2 January, the Queen,

wearing a ceremonial Kiwi feather cloak, urged her Maori subjects to hold fast to their own language and culture. Arriving in New Plymouth by train, she attended a memorable rally of 18,000 in the natural amphitheatre of Pukekura Park, weaving in and out of ranks of excited children in her landrover. Moving on to South Island she reached Wellington the capital, a city built on a circle of hills around one of the world's finest deep water harbours, on 16 January. To open the New Zealand Parliament the Queen wore her Coronation dress and thus carried maple leaves and wheat and jute and the other Commonwealth emblems into the Antipodean legislative chamber. The Duke was in full dress naval uniform. The opening was a magnificent occasion and it was New Zealand's own. Earlier at a luncheon Her Majesty had referred to the country as this "rich and lovely land". In her speech she also restated her belief in the Commonwealth, calling it "one of the great forces of good in the world, and the arduous times in which we live are a challenge to us to exert that beneficent influence with telling effect". In Christchurch she set a new precedent by holding an investiture and conferring a knighthood in public.

Being an entire continent with a much larger population, Australia was a more arduous prospect for the Queen than New Zealand. Her stay there was a two-month one. She reached Sydney on 3 February. As in New Zealand, she was the first reigning monarch in history to tour the Commonwealth of Australia. Fittingly a million and a half of her fellow countrymen lined ten miles of Sydney streets to welcome the Queen of Australia, the warmest welcome coming from those in working-class quarters. The Queen opened the New South Wales Legislature and bestowed honours on 127 men and 13 women in the ballroom of Government House. Australian sport, Australian literature, Australian music—Her Majesty sampled them all during her tour

On 13 February, before going to the other five Australian states, the Queen proceeded to Canberra, the spacious but still incomplete federal capital, for four days. The State Opening of the Australian Parliament was of course the highlight of the visit. "It is a joy for me today" the Queen told members "to address you not as a Queen from far away, but as your Queen and a part of your Parliament". For a children's rally at Manuka Oval she wore a dress of wattle yellow—wattle being the Australian national flower—and a hat made of wattle sprigs and grey-green

foliage. After the Queen's broadcast from the state banquet, in which she expressed her positive impressions of the country, a woman commented "You know, I've always talked about Australia as being a grand place, but I've never really felt it until the Queen spoke".

The Queen and Duke boarded the *Gothic* again for the journey to Tasmania, arriving 20 February in Hobart on its 150th anniversary. Later she flew to Northern Tasmania where little girls in Dutch costume, representative of the increasingly multicultural nature of Australian society, sang a song of welcome. Tasmania was followed by Victoria and its capital Melbourne. Here the Queen opened another state parliament. During a brief rest at O'Shannassy Lodge in the Great Dividing Range mountains, she and the Duke became acquainted with the real Australian bush. Then there was the long flight to Brisbane, capital

17,000 children greeted the Queen of Australia on Melbourne's cricket ground, 4 March 1954.

A radiant Queen, wearing on her dress yellow wattle, Australia's floral emblem, leaves the state banquet in Sydney accompanied by the Premier of New South Wales, J.J. Cahill.

March. Four youngsters came 2,000 miles from Port Darwin in the Northern Territory just to see their Queen there. On a visit to the industrial centre of Whyalla, Her Majesty saw Aboriginal dances never before seen by a white woman. The visit to Woomera by the Duke of Edinburgh carried more sinister associations. It was the testing ground for rockets and atomic weapons under a joint Australian-United Kingdom programme. An outbreak of polio threatened the Queen's visit to Perth and Western Australia from 27 to 30 March but it was salvaged when the Queen reluctantly agreed not to shake hands with anyone presented to her. The outdoor ball given by the Lord Mayor of Perth at the city's university was voted the most glamorous of the tour.

On 1 April the Queen and Duke sailed from Fremantle. As their white ship made its way into the westering sun, escorted by an aircraft carrier and several cruisers, thousands watched from the shore. But stocktaking began even before the departure. The historian of the 1953–54 royal tour wrote that it was agreed that the Queen of Australia's tour "revealed to the world the splendour of Australia's achievement and to Australians themselves the opportunities ahead of them for building a noble future". From the cabin of the *Gothic*, the Queen broadcast her farewell message. "Our thanks go to you all for

of the vast state of Queensland, on 9 March. Though it was the rainy season, the weather proved favourable, and the Queen also flew to Bundaberg and to Toowoomba where she saw the Australian Aborigines perform their corroboree dances. At Cairns, the farthest north the Queen reached, Her Majesty reboarded the *Gothic* for a visit to the Great Barrier Reef and spent the day on Seaforth Island, one of the Cumberland group of smaller islands and reefs. When the Queen left Queensland on 18 March she had chalked up 1,000 flying miles in that state alone.

The royal party used Adelaide as the centre for the tour of South Australia from 19 to 25

your welcome, your hospitality and your loyalty" she said. "And now I say goodbye—God be with you—until the next time I can visit Australia."

On its long journey eastwards to Ceylon across the Indian Ocean, the *Gothic* stopped briefly at the Cocos-Keeling Islands. On 10 April, Elizabeth II, Queen of Ceylon, made her ceremonial entry into Colombo, the capital, with all the splendour of the ancient Sinhalese Kings of the island. The heat was intense the next day—so much so the glass beads on the Queen's dress were scorching—when, to the sound of conch shells and drums, Her Majesty, once again in her rich Coronation dress, opened the Ceylonese Parliament. Cooler air refreshed Her Majesty and His Royal Highness as they left the plains for the hills of central Ceylon. The climax of their stay was the Raja Perahera, the great procession in Kandy. A crowd of a million watched 140 magnificently decked elephants and gorgeously dressed spinning and whirling dancers move through the streets to the Temple accompanied by trumpets and drums. There in the sacred city the Queen saw the tooth of Buddha, the most sacred relic of the Buddhist world.

The *Gothic* was now on its return voyage but the Queen's work was by no means complete. A warm welcome awaited her and the Duke on 27 April in Aden at the tip of the Arabian Peninsula. Aden was important for Com-

monwealth defence so there were military parades and the Duke visited an oil refinery under construction. The royal couple then boarded a flight to Uganda in east Africa. Pressing a button the Queen opened the Owen Falls Dam on the Nile below Lake Victoria, Nyanza for a new hydro electric scheme. Political difficulties shortened the tour programme, so on 1 May the Queen and Duke flew to Tobruk where they boarded the newly commissioned Royal Yacht *Britannia* for an ecstatic welcome

The Queen arrived to open her Ceylon Parliament in weather so hot the beading on her dress was scorching.

from their children Prince Charles and Princess Anne. The *Britannia* headed for Malta escorted by the Mediterranean Fleet commanded by the Duke of Edinburgh's uncle Lord Mountbatten. Bells of the city and the crackle of fireworks heralded Her Majesty's arrival in the harbour. On the mall before the walls of Valetta the Queen unveiled a memorial to the 2,301 officers and men of the Commonwealth Air Forces killed in defence of Malta in World War II. Her Majesty spent five days in Malta renewing old acquaintances from the days of her life there as the wife of a naval officer when the Duke was in command of HMS *Magpie*.

Gibraltar on 10 May, where Prince Charles and Princess Anne were fascinated by the Rock's most famous inhabitants, the Barbary apes, was the last stop of the tour. When *Britannia* finally entered the Channel, hundreds of small ships came out to escort the Queen into United Kingdom waters, the final leg of the journey. Up the Thames she sailed to Westminster where she and the Duke disembarked on 15 May for the drive back to Buckingham Palace through wildly cheering London crowds.

Two years and three months had passed since the Queen succeeded to her scattered thrones. She was now crowned and had just wrapped up a triumphant progress around the world, taking possession of several of those realms on four different continents. Into that short period had been packed drama, splendour and exposure for the Sovereign. The world tour was not a planned part of the succession scenario but had proved an exceptionally effective presentation to the globe of the new Queen Elizabeth II.

The Queen in turn imprinted her image on the Commonwealth. First impressions are important. Had she waited longer to do this, it might have taken more time to become the great world figure she now clearly was. Her trip also made the world aware of the Commonwealth as opposed to the British Empire. Though it had been born in 1931, the Commonwealth had not quite been taken in by the public mind. Now it was. Also in these two years the Queen made clear to everyone that the Commonwealth was one of her priorities and interests. She herself had got to know it at first hand, particularly the new Commonwealth, and to understand some of its problems. How she would build on this auspicious opening of her reign, what leadership she would provide and how she would fulfil her promise of service would be the story of the rest of the reign.

Elizabeth II Wears the Crown They Wore

Queen Elizabeth II is the thirty-third Monarch to reign over Canada. She is descended from, or in other ways closely related to, all the Kings and Queens who came before her, French-speaking and English-speaking. Though divided by rivalries of settlement, war and religion, the two lines of Canada's Monarchs frequently intermarried and as a result were really one large family. Here are some of these famous Monarchs of Canada's history.

Queen Elizabeth II, first of the 33 Monarchs to bear the title Queen of Canada. An official picture taken by John Evans after Her Majesty opened Parliament in Ottawa in 1977. The Queen is wearing the insignia of the Order of the Garter founded in 1348 and the Sovereign's Badge of one of her newest honours, the Order of Canada, established by her in 1967. The fringes of her dress, suggestive of an aboriginal princess, suit a Monarch given the name Ar Oh Muthl or Mother of All Peoples by the Salish in 1959.

Queen Elizabeth I on Newfoundland's 1933 stamp to mark its Sir Humphrey Gilbert celebrations. She financed Frobisher's search for the Northwest Passage, gave Gilbert a Royal Charter to settle Newfoundland and named the mainland 'Meta Incognita'. Elizabeth II quoted her illustrious predecessor when opening Parliament in Ottawa in 1957.

In the 1670 painting at the Ursuline Convent, Quebec City, entitled "La France apportant la foi aux Hurons", Queen Anne, Consort of King Louis XIII and mother of King Louis XIV, is depicted standing on the Banks of the St Lawrence River.

Charles II shown on one of the most important documents of Canadian history —the Royal Charter of the Hudson's Bay Company granted by the King in 1670.

King George V, Silver Jubilee window, St James' Cathedral, Toronto. George V adopted Royal Arms for Canada and enacted the Statute of Westminster establishing Canada's legal independence. From 1931 he was King of Canada separately from being Sovereign of the United Kingdom, Australia, etc., and became the first legal Canadian as Canadian Citizenship was not created until 1947.

Queen Anne receives the four Indian Kings at Court in 1710. A window in Her Majesty's Chapel of the Mohawk, Brantford, Ontario. The Queen gave the Mohawks the historic Communion Plate which is one of Canada's great cultural treasures.

Portrait at the University of St Michael's College, Toronto, thought to be King James II. As Duke of York, James II was the Hudson's Bay Company's second Governor. He secured his brother King Charles II's agreement that the Company's charter applied to the inland territory of Canada as well as the coastal waters of the Bay.

King William IV, first member of the Royal Family in Canada, 1786. After becoming King in 1830, he sent this portrait of himself to the Nova Scotia Legislature.

King Edward VIII at the unveiling of the Vimy Memorial in France 1936. Inauguration of the great monument to the dead of Canada's battle of nationhood in World War I was the only external engagement the King carried out in his eleven-month reign.

Graceful silhouettes of King George VI and Queen Elizabeth (now Queen Mother) adorn the lion monument at the Toronto end of Ontario's Queen Elizabeth Way. The parents of Elizabeth II were the first reigning monarchs to tour Canada in 1939.

Tribute by THE GLOBE to Queen Victoria near the end of her reign. Victoria, great-great grandmother of Elizabeth II, chose Ottawa as Canada's capital, proclaimed Confederation, named British Columbia and the City of New Westminster and chose the pitcher plant as Newfoundland's floral emblem. She has been called the "Mother of Confederation".

Statue of King Louis XIV, Place Royale, Quebec City. By making Quebec a Royal Province in 1663, Louis XIV made certain that a viable French-speaking community would exist in North America.

King George IV grants the Royal Charter of what is now the University of Toronto 1826. Detail from W. Scott Carter's 1937 map at Hart House, Toronto.

Canadian Mohawks receiving copies of the Book of Common Prayer, *translated into Mohawk by Joseph Brant, from the hands of King George III and Queen Charlotte, 1787*

Heads of King Henry VII (top left) and King François I (above left), who sent Giovanni Caboto and Jacques Cartier on their voyages of discovery in 1497 and 1534 and founded the two lines of monarchs who have reigned in Canada, are carved over the doors of the House of Commons in Ottawa.

Statue of King Edward VII in Montreal by the sculptor Louis Hébert. It is inscribed "Hommage au roi pacificateur".

King George II on a medal given by him to aboriginal chiefs in Canada. National Archives of Canada.

5

A New Elizabethan Age

1955–1963

State portraits of the Queen and Duke of Edinburgh commissioned by the Canadian Government and completed in 1956. They hang in the ballroom of Rideau Hall.

The Queen's golden age. That is how the 1950's appear when looked back on from the fiftieth year of her reign—years seemingly free from the social, political and personal turmoil of later decades. The truth is otherwise. The glamour and excitement of Elizabeth II's Coronation and world tour have obscured the whirlwind of crises and problems that arose the moment she ascended the Throne and continued for most of the decade.

The Queen's very accession brought serious family problems. How was she to handle the abrupt ending of her husband's promising naval career? The Duke of Edinburgh had all the makings of a First Sea Lord. Had King George VI lived several years more, Philip could have achieved that ambition, but as husband of the reigning

Changes brought about by the Queen's Accession meant that the Duke of Edinburgh had to create a new role for himself as the husband of the Queen. Arriving for the first meeting of the Coronation Commission which he chaired.

became his wife's private secretary, so well informed about state affairs, politics and diplomacy that the two were almost joint Monarchs. Wise enough not to try to copy his ancestor, the Duke of Edinburgh would never be content with inactivity either. He was a man of intelligence, independence and integrity. The Queen would find the range of talent he possessed a real asset. Since his marriage to Elizabeth four years before he had been head of the family. Now that position was ignored and everyone went instead to the Queen for everything—because of course she *was* the Queen. Equally devastating to the Queen and Duke was the necessity of leaving the home they had so quickly and lovingly created at Clarence House— the first real home the Duke ever had —to reside in Buckingham Palace.

Fortunately for the Queen, the Duke did find his way. He worked it out and she was patient and understanding while he did. His strategy was to distance himself from the Queen's constitutional duties and functions. He concentrated on his role as husband and father. From this standpoint he was better able to help the Queen, dealing with problems a man may find it easier to handle than a woman, tackling matters that would save his wife time and energy. It was he who dealt with the royal estates for instance. At this time too he began to develop the many interests with which he would long be identified. Keeping slightly apart from his wife's regality, he could act as her sounding board in public, express things the Queen would like to say

Monarch he had to give up a profession that might conflict with the services expected of the Queen's spouse. "He hated leaving a life in which he was so thoroughly happy" wrote his valet John Dean of this reluctant sacrifice. What exactly the Duke would now do was not clear, for the role of male consort of a Queen regnant is no more laid out than is the job of the Monarch's heir.

He had no inclination to follow the example of Queen Victoria's husband Prince Albert who but could not, or reach sections of the Commonwealth public the Queen would find it hard to touch.

Finding his way was not easy and he had to put up with many slights. Stirred up by learning that the Duke's uncle Lord Mountbatten was telling people the House of Mountbatten was now on the Throne, Queen Mary got Churchill formally to advise the Queen that her family name should continue to be Windsor, not the Duke's adopted surname Mountbatten. The Queen made a declaration to this effect to the Privy Council. Removal of the consort's throne from the House of Lords and substitution of a chair of estate on a lower level for him, was another insult resented by the Duke. The royal couple's changed status was a jolt to both of them and the fact that they worked it out indicates the love, understanding and trust that existed in their union. Later the Queen was able to show her gratitude to her husband publicly for his part in resolving the problems. On 22 February 1957 she made the Duke—by birth a Prince of Greece and Denmark—a Prince of the United Kingdom and Northern Ireland.

Coming to the Throne when her children, Prince Charles and Princess Anne, needed their mother most, posed another dilemma for the Queen. The duties of Monarch severely limited the time she could give them. She had to leave the children entirely for over five months to make the 1953–54 Commonwealth tour just as her parents had left her in 1927. While she was absent Prince Charles learned to read. The Queen was deprived of the pleasure of teaching her son the way her mother had taught her. What she was doing was balancing the claims of work and family as any professional woman has to.

The Duke emerges from an Inuit dwelling during his 1954 solo tour of the Canadian North.

Fortunately, Elizabeth II's mother was at hand and ready to care for the two grandchildren. Here was another potential family problem that happily worked itself out. Widowed at 51, deprived of her role as Queen Consort in the prime of life, Queen Elizabeth the Queen Mother might well have retired from public view and at first seemed to be doing so. But once recovered from the shock of the King's death, her steely character, common sense and love of life reasserted themselves. She re-emerged to develop a special role of her own as Queen Mother, a role for many years of no small help to her daughter Elizabeth II.

Another family crisis burst unexpectedly on the Queen a week after the Coronation. A British tabloid called *The People* broke the story that Princess Margaret was in love with a divorced man and wished to marry him. This situation had been developing since 1948. During the war, King George VI came up with the seemingly good idea of appointing war heroes as equerries at the Palace, instead of people from the old noble families. One of them was a handsome and charming group captain named Peter Townsend, hero of the Battle of Britain. Unfortunately, no one told the new equerry that part of his job was to avoid falling in love with members of the Royal Family. Townsend's wartime marriage had foundered and he obtained a divorce in 1951 when his wife left him. He fitted in well at the Palace and the Royal Family became tremendously fond of him. Princess Margaret, grieving and lonely from her father's death, found him a ready and sympathetic consoler. Townsend's new appointment as Comptroller of the Queen Mother's Household meant he continued to be close to the Queen's sister.

Townsend declared his love to Princess Margaret just before the Coronation. Princess Margaret immediately informed the Queen. The new Monarch was faced with an appalling predicament. No wonder the Queen Mother burst into tears on learning about what seemed like a replay of the Abdication crisis. Elizabeth II wanted her sister, of whom she had been protective from the first, to be happy. But as temporal Governor of the Church of England, how could she condone a breech of the Church's marriage laws—even when Townsend had been the innocent party in his divorce? The Queen asked Princess Margaret and Townsend to wait a year. Under the Royal Marriages Act Princess Margaret, until she reached the age of twenty-five, had to have the Queen's and Parliament's consent to marry. After that she could wed without it if she gave the Privy Council twelve months' notice of her intention. But by taking that course she would lose her royal status and income voted by Parliament.

Emotion pulled the Queen one way, duty another, but as Monarch she felt compelled to act as her governments wished. Although no ministerial advice was actually sought, the cabinets of her Commonwealth realms were all sounded out informally. The consensus was that the marriage was not acceptable. Memories of the Abdication were too fresh, the public was not prepared to accept divorce at the top. Townsend was transferred to Brussels as air attaché and Princess Margaret flew to Rhodesia for a tour with the Queen Mother. Because Princess Margaret mistakenly got the idea that government approval of the marriage might be forthcoming after she reached twenty-five, the crisis dragged on unresolved until 1955.

Following the Princess's twenty-fifth birthday and Townsend's reappearance, the news media whipped up an hysteria of speculation about the question harmful to the Crown. The Queen, determined not to press her sister one way or the other, avoided any discussion of the situation with Margaret until almost the last minute. Finally, on 31 October 1955, Princess Margaret issued a statement. "I have decided not to marry Group Captain Peter Townsend" she said. "Mindful of the Church's teaching that Christian marriage is indissoluble, and conscious of my duty to the Commonwealth, I have resolved to put these considerations before any others".

Writing about the crisis, Elizabeth Longford concluded that the young Queen Elizabeth II had a lot to learn about people. Her maturity in her work was not matched by similar skill in understanding what people thought and felt. That would come with experience. Sarah Bradford, a 1996 biographer of Her Majesty, agrees. The Queen "as a wise and kind human being …

Elizabeth II, Queen of Canada and Head of the Commonwealth, addresses the United Nations General Assembly, New York, 1957. As a busy professional, the Queen had to balance the demands of her family and her job.

played for time, refusing to pressurise her sister, insisting that Margaret make her own decision". But perhaps being unkind and telling her the marriage was impossible would have ended the crisis sooner and left the principals less scarred.

In learning to be Queen on the job, Elizabeth II had other personal adjustments to make too, some undreamt of by the public. For one thing people expected a smiling Queen. But to hold a smile all the way along a processional route is a physical impossibility. "You get a twitch" explained one of the Queen's ladies-in-

waiting "so there is a moment when you have to relax your muscles" and for that moment you are not smiling. When this happened the Queen would always catch the voice of someone in the crowd calling out "How cross she's looking!" Being under constant gaze was also a great strain to get used to.

It was in the 1950's Elizabeth II had her first trouble with the media. In developing his support role for the Queen, the Duke went on several long Commonwealth tours. The media at once started up rumours of a marital break up between the Queen and him. Major incidents of that kind occurred in 1956 and 1957 and were so serious an official denial had to be issued. Two articles critical of the Sovereign caused a stir in 1957. Lord Altrincham, a minor publisher-editor, accused the Queen's official speeches of being like those "of a priggish schoolgirl, captain of the hockey team, a prefect and a recent candidate for Confirmation" and called her voice "a pain in the neck". Then on the eve of the Thanksgiving weekend in Ottawa, *Saturday Evening Post*, a New York publication, reproduced an article called "the Royal Soap Opera" by the British writer Malcolm Muggeridge who said the Monarchy was a substitute for real religion. An uproar resulted. Though the Queen was not the writers' main object—Altrincham was attacking the British establishment, Muggeridge twentieth century materialism—this criticism was not constructive advice helping her improve the Monarchy but an unjustified assault by self-appointed critics on an public person who was certainly performing up to scratch. As Sarah Bradford later pointed out, the communications media was rapidly becoming the screen through which the Queen was interpreted to her peoples. It did not take Her Majesty long to realise the need to reach through the screen and make direct contact with her subjects.

Barely two years after returning from the 1953–54 Commonwealth tour, the Queen was confronted with the Suez crisis. In response to Egypt's violation of treaty rights by its nationalisation of the Suez Canal and the failure of the United Nations to provide redress, the United Kingdom and France arranged for Israel to attack Egypt so that they could intervene militarily in the Canal zone on the pretext of separating the antagonists. The affair ended in an ignominious Anglo-French retreat. Throughout the crisis the Queen's position "was absolutely constitutional and impartial" though it seems doubtful her United Kingdom Prime Minister, Sir Anthony Eden, kept her fully informed of his schemes. In addition to the damage done to her British realm, the Queen was faced with a Commonwealth split—India and Canada opposed the United Kingdom action—that weakened the family and undid much of the good achieved by her tour.

The year after Suez came the resignation of the British Prime Minister. Her Majesty had to choose his successor, Harold Macmillan. A political turnabout occurred in Canada that year too. After being in office since 1935, the Liberal Party was rejected by the electorate and a minority Conservative Government took office. The Queen's work as Queen of Canada meanwhile unfolded daily. Her first return to Canada as Queen was that middle of the night stop at Gander in 1953. Four years later, she went to Ottawa for Thanksgiving to meet her Canadian Parliament. But tours were just part of the job. Elizabeth II touched her Canadian subjects in many other ways. Just days after becoming Queen she received the retiring Governor-General of Canada, Field Marshal Lord Alexander in audience. Alexander "was able to give the Queen the latest news from the Dominion, including the development of public thought that more and more placed the Queen in the personal role of Queen of Canada, which was expressed in suggestions that she should visit the Dominion more frequently and maintain a permanent establishment there where she could spend long periods of full time residence".

In 1952 the Queen bestowed the title 'Royal' on Winnipeg's up-and-coming ballet company, the first outside the United Kingdom to be honoured by her. At the end of July 1954 she saw the Duke off on a solo tour of Canada. This 10,000 mile trip enabled him to visit the North and see much of the scientific and industrial work Canadians were doing. In a radio broadcast from Yellowknife on 10 August he revealed that "like many boys, I read stories about Canada's North-West and I have long had the ambition to see what it looked like". Philip was starting the record he would establish as the member of the Royal Family to have travelled in Canada more often than any other in history. The Consort with a small "c" could act as eyes and ears for the Queen. Already in 1951 his keen mind had challenged platitudes about the country. The frequent description of Canada as "a young country", implying as it did inexperience and lack of judgement, he told Canadians then, did not "fit a nation that drove a railroad through the Rockies, developed the prairies, and exploited the vast natural resources of timber, oil and water power, and is steadily pushing the last frontier northward".

Separate institutions for the Canadian Crown continued to develop. In 1954 the Queen chose a cap badge for The Canadian Guards, the new unit created when the Canadian Army was expanded to meet the commitments of the Korean War. Because the Queen had now taken the title Queen of Canada, the Chief of the General Staff, Lieut.-General Guy

Simonds, felt that Her Majesty should have a Household Regiment in the regular forces which would recruit nationally instead of locally and be bilingual. In 1956 Her Majesty approved new coats-of-arms for the Yukon and Northwest Territories. That year too the state portraits of the Queen and the Duke commissioned by the Canadian Government were completed by the Montreal artist Lilias Torrance Newton. The following year Her Majesty approved the change of colour of the maple leaves in the Royal Arms of Canada from green to red (this is the source of the colours of the National Flag adopted in 1965).

On 14 November 1955 the Queen authorised the new Great Seal of Canada for her reign. Designed by Canadian artist Eric Aldwinckel and engraved by Thomas Shingles, the Great Seal, 135 mm in diameter, was a magnificent creation following the classic practice of monarchy. It showed Elizabeth II crowned, holding sceptre and orb and enthroned above the Royal Arms of Canada and encircled by the words "Reine du Canada / Elizabeth II / Queen of Canada". Two years later, in 1957, the Queen approved the fixing of the celebration of her official birthday in Canada permanently on Victoria Day, Canada's oldest civic holiday. (It is Canada's best kept secret that Victoria Day celebrates the birthday of the reigning monarch and that artillery salutes across the land that day are for Elizabeth II and not Victoria.)

Had more attention been paid to the Queen's problems in her early years on the Throne, there would have been less hyperbole about Elizabeth II's reign as the new Elizabethan Age. The '50's even at a glance bore little resemblance to the Tudor era. The Queen herself was like the great Elizabeth in just two ways—her name and the fact that both Queens came to the Throne at age 25. Nevertheless, Elizabethan themes surfaced in Coronation and tour decorations and for years afterwards figures

The Queen prepares to leave Oporto at the end of her triumphant state visit to Portugal 1957.

in flamboyant Elizabethan dress—Raleighs, Shakespeares, Frobishers and Bacons—cropped up in commercial advertisements. This fantasizing was of little help to the Queen in finding her feet. In fact it seems to have annoyed her—judging at least from her allusion to it in the 1953 Christmas broadcast from New Zealand. "Frankly" she said "I do not myself feel at all like my great Tudor forbear, who was blessed with neither husband nor children, who ruled as a despot and was never able to leave her native shores".

Problems at home in the Commonwealth were counterbalanced for the Queen by the success of her visits to foreign countries during her first decade as Monarch. She had begun the state visits that in fifty years were to make her a well-known figure on every continent and the most travelled monarch in world history. In February 1957 she went to Portugal, the country that an accident of history made a republic but one whose people were monarchist at heart. April the same year saw the Queen in Paris where the crowds were so enthusiastic they had to be kept back by mounted guards with drawn swords. And in May she went to visit her kinsman, King Frederik IX of Denmark, who, incidentally, was also head of her husband's family, the house of Schleswig-Holstein-Sonderburg-Glucksburg.

In 1951 and 1957 the Queen saw that Canada was a land of dreams, though she may not have realised how long term the dreams tended to be. One Canadian dream, dating from the seventeenth century, was to provide access for ocean going ships to the Great Lake system via the St Lawrence River. Canals and small locks bypassing the natural obstacles such the Lachine Rapids and Niagara Falls had existed

for a couple of centuries. The Welland Canal had been rebuilt as recently as the post World War I period but the United States, with whom Canada shared the system of lakes and rivers, was reluctant to rebuild the Montreal and Lake Ontario channels. Finally in 1951 the Canadian Government threatened to build a seaway entirely within Canadian territory. This finally produced a joint agreement between the two countries in 1954.

The St Lawrence Seaway, as the project was called, was finished in 1959 after four-and-a-half years, the greatest engineering feat to that date in North America. To open it as Queen of Canada, together with President Dwight Eisenhower, the American head of state, was the purpose of Elizabeth II's big 1959 tour. The Queen and the Duke landed at Torbay, Newfoundland on 18 June and were met by the Governor-General, Vincent Massey. The royal couple made their way to the capital, St John's, where they spent the night at Government House and were taken on a tour of the Confederation Building by the Premier, Joey Smallwood.

Soon after their arrival in St John's, the Queen's doctor confirmed what she already thought and hoped—that she was going to have another child. The Queen confided the good news to her Prime Minister, John Diefenbaker, who for the rest of his life took great pride in having been the first public official in the Commonwealth to be told. Here was shared monarchy working as it should. Not for a moment did the Queen think of cancelling the tour, though its strenuous itinerary would tax her strength to the maximum in the six-and-a-half weeks and 18,000 miles that lay ahead.

"This occasion deserves a place in history." Speaking at the opening of the St Lawrence Seaway 26 June 1959.

Next day Her Majesty flew to Gander to open the International Airport before going on to Corner Brook, to tour the Bowater Paper Mill, and to Stephenville. She and the Duke took to the air again on 20 June for a flight to Schefferville in the east central part of Labrador. Then it was south to Sept Iles, Quebec, on the north shore of the St Lawrence, where they boarded *Britannia* and sailed to Gaspé. At this scenic town on 21 June the Queen attended a ceremony at the Jacques Cartier Memorial Cross, laying a bouquet of thirty-six red roses at the granite cross commemorating the explorer's arrival in 1534. As it was Sunday, she went to service at St Paul's Church.

Up the St Lawrence sailed the *Britannia* bearing the Sovereign of Canada on her historic mission. Before reaching the ancient capital of Quebec, there was a side trip into the Saguenay River—its name redolent of the early explorers' Kingdom of the Saguenay—to Arvida and Chicoutimi. At Chicoutimi, Mayor Rosaire Gauthier presented Her Majesty with a painting

by local artist René Richard. In Quebec City on 23 June cheering crowds broke through police barriers and brought the royal car to a halt. On the Plains of Abraham, the Queen presented colours to her regiment the Royal 22e Régiment, visited Marguerite Bourgeoys girls' school and at night attended a provincial dinner at the Chateau Frontenac given by the Premier, the aging Maurice Duplessis. There she made the first speech of her tour. "Demeurez donc fidèles à vos traditions et à votre culture", she urged French-speaking Canadians, "et contribuez ainsi à la grandeur de votre pays".

After a stop at Trois Rivières to visit Le Flambeau monument, the Queen and Duke reached Montreal on 25 June where a packed programme awaited them. It included an official welcome at the Champs de Mars, a visit to handicapped children in John Cabot Park and a big civic ball in the evening. Next day came the highlight of the tour. On 26 June, the Queen, accompanied by the Prime Minister and Mrs Diefenbaker, met the American President,

Dwight Eisenhower, and Mrs Eisenhower, at the Royal Canadian Air Force station St Hubert. They drove with them to the site of the opening ceremonies.

In her speech the Queen welcomed the United States President to Canada. As Allied Supreme Commander in World War II, he had been well known to the Royal Family and stayed with them at Balmoral Castle. "We can say in truth", the Queen noted of the day's event, "that this occasion deserves a place in history". She traced the dream of the St Lawrence Seaway to Dollier de Casson, who in 1680 conceived the idea of surmounting the Lachine Rapids. She pointed out that the new waterway would affect the lives of generations of both their peoples. Praising the politicians, engineers and workmen who made it possible, she extended to them "my congratulations and the congratulations of their fellow citizens". The co-operative effort, she said, also exemplified the enduring friendship of Canada and the United States. "That partnership is most agreeably symbolised, Mr President, in the fact that you and I

have joined together to perform this ceremony today" she added.

In response, President Eisenhower told Her Majesty that the opening of the Seaway gave him the chance to express "the lasting respect, admiration, and affection of the citizens of the

Britannia *enters the ceremonial gates, made of timbers from the old Lachine Canal, at the St Lambert Lock, officially opening the St Lawrence Seaway. The Seaway had been unofficially open since April.*

The Queen and President Eisenhower from the bridge of the Britannia *observe those watching them as they make their way through the Seaway following the official opening.*

United States for you and all the people of Canada over whom you reign". The ceremony over, the Monarch and the Head of State boarded *Britannia* and at the St Lambert Lock sailed through a ceremonial gate created out of old logs from the Lachine Canal to open the Seaway officially. *Britannia* was actually the 425th ship to pass through the Seaway which had been open unofficially since April. Church bells rang, ships hooted and bands played as the Royal Yacht then made its way up the St Lawrence towards Kingston. There were stops for additional Seaway ceremonies at the

Her Majesty begins the dancing with Sarto Fournier, Mayor of Montreal, at the big civic ball given by the city in her honour at the Queen Elizabeth Hotel, 25 June 1959.

anything but tame. He told Canadians they were out of shape, citing figures that showed only 34% of the male population of military age could pass an armed forces medical. To remedy this he urged his fellow countrymen to see there was "proper physical education in schools, adequate recreational facilities for all ages and sections of the community, an extension of the work of youth organisations both in scope and age, and finally an organisation to publicise sports and recreational activities and to encourage people to take part in them". He mentioned the contribution his recently established Duke of Edinburgh's Award was making in this regard. Considerable resentment was expressed over the Duke's speech at the time but it proved a watershed and played its role in setting Canadians jogging, cycling, and exercising in the decades ahead.

Moses-Saunders Power Dam and the Robert H. Saunders St Lawrence Generating Station. At the latter Her Majesty was joined by the American Vice-President, Richard Nixon and Governor Rockefeller of New York State.

At Kingston on 28 June, the Queen attended service at Sydenham Street United Church and visited Fort Henry. In Toronto there was a civic reception and a Ball at the Royal York Hotel, and the Sovereign attended her first Queen's Plate. Here the Duke took centre stage as he was installed as the first ever lay President of the Canadian Medical Association on 30 June. His Royal Highness's presidential speech was

Chinese Canadians greet the Queen at the civic reception in Richardson Stadium, Kingston, Ontario.

Elizabeth II sees "The Golden Mile", Scarborough, the first shopping plaza in Canada.

Chicago gave the Queen and Duke a tremendous ovation with over 2,000,000 people on the streets to catch a glimpse of them.

From Toronto the Queen flew to Ottawa for her first Dominion Day. Since it was her third stay at Government House, she could describe Rideau Hall as "this my home in Ottawa" in a real as well as a technical sense, as she did in her Dominion Day broadcast to the country. Her Majesty held an investiture at Government House, presented regimental colours on Parliament Hill, unveiled a striking memorial to the dead of Commnwealth Air Forces who served in Canada but whose graves are unknown and was host of a dinner to which the country's current hockey idol 'Rocket' Richard was invited.

After Ottawa there were visits to cities in southwestern Ontario. At the Stratford Festival which had been founded the year of her accession, the Queen attended a performance of *As You Like It*. In Windsor a quarter of a million people jammed the tour route and watched her board *Britannia*, with the Detroit skyline and a third of a million

Making her way to her first Dominion Day on Parliament Hill, 1 July 1959.

111

Americans watching from across the river in the background. On her way to the upper lakes the Queen stopped to visit Muskoka. But the day in Chicago was her real triumph. She arrived there and was welcomed as Queen of Canada, with Diefenbaker her Minister in Attendance, on 6 July. At least two million people lined the streets of this reputedly isolationist and anti-monarchist city and gave her a terrific reception.

When *Britannia* reached Port Arthur (now Thunder Bay) on 9 July, Her Majesty flew from there to Calgary for the western part of her tour. There she attended her second Stampede before going on to Banff, Vernon and Kamloops. She reached Vancouver on 15 July and opened its Deas Island Tunnel, connecting the city with its surrounding suburbs under the Fraser River. British Columbia had arranged an extensive welcome in the capital, Victoria. It included a garden party for 4,000 at Government House and a dinner and ball. In a stunning evening dress of jade green and turquoise blue flowered taffeta with full gathered back, Her Majesty danced with one of her future Prime Ministers, John Turner. Formality and informality alternated. When the Leader of the Opposition was presented and the Duke found there were three opposition parties in the provincial Legislature, he asked him why they did not get together and defeat the government. "Don't give him ideas" quipped the colourful Premier, W.A.C. Bennett. The Royal Canadian Navy's farewell salute to the Queen on the other hand included a display

Artist George Paginton's painting of Britannia *making its way through the Welland Canal on its journey to the upper Great Lakes.*

Visiting an Aboriginal community at Nanaimo, British Columbia.

to Edmonton on 20 July and resumed her engagements the next day. It was a whistle stop journey across the Prairies to Saskatoon, Regina and then Winnipeg. One highlight was the Queen's visit to the 640 acre mixed farm of Mr and Mrs Carl Wells on 22 July. After touring the barnyard, the Queen and Duke had tea with their hosts. "I felt very comfortable and relaxed with them" Mrs Wells said afterwards. From Winnipeg Her Majesty flew to Sudbury for what one journalist called a "hometown hero" welcome. She went down the Frood Nickel Mine which twenty years before her mother Queen Elizabeth had been the first woman to visit.

After a two day rest for the royal couple at Batterwood, Vincent Massey's country house near Port Hope, the tour ended with visits to Fredericton on 27 July, followed by Saint John,

of fireworks and twelve ships all formally illuminated, stretching from Finlayson Point to Shoal Bay.

People had begun to notice the Queen was tired from time to time on the tour No one knew that she was pregnant so there was criticism of tour organisers for making her itinerary too strenuous—the Canadian habit of throwing extras in once the basic structure was set. When she flew to Whitehorse on 18 July she felt unwell enough to take a two day rest, thereby missing Dawson, Yellowknife and Uranium City which the Duke visited alone. By now many suspected the real cause of Her Majesty's indisposition but her entourage refused to confirm the rumours.

From Whitehorse she flew direct

In Vancouver the Queen opened the theatre named in her honour.

Crown used to decorate the Ontario Legislature during the 1959 tour.

ance could not be faulted. Of course there were always ways for improvement. Ottawa's *Le Droit* justly (and ominously) complained that "Le discours que la reine prononça à l'occasion de l'inauguration de la Voie maritime... ne fut pas non plus officiellement traduit en français". But it did not blame the Queen. On the contrary, its editorial of 2 July noted how "Sa Majesté fait rougir (où devrait faire rougir) ces milliers des Canadiens qui, pour une raison où pour une autre, s'opposent encore à l'enseignement et à la diffusion du français; elle fait rougir aussi tous ces Canadiens d'origine française qui ont honte de leur langue maternelle, qui l'abandonnent où qui la corrompent". But the overall impact was positive. The Canadian Monarchy was on track. "We can be grateful" wrote Leonard Brockington in *The Globe Magazine*, 1 August, "that two of our young fellow Canadians, Elizabeth and Philip, have walked among us in gentleness, understanding and compassion".

Moncton and Shediac. A flying visit to Prince Edward Island included a tour of the Brackley farm of Mr and Mrs Willard Prowse. Before departing from Halifax by plane, the Queen attended a meeting of the federal Cabinet, at which she approved the appointment of the distinguished soldier, Major-General Georges Vanier, as Governor-General of Canada. At the federal-provincial dinner at the Nova Scotian Hotel, she was able to thank Vincent Massey for his services in representing her in Canada since 1952.

The Queen had made clear when the tour was in the planning stage that the one thing she insisted on was meeting the people. This she had done. She had also enjoyed the tour and felt it was the most interesting and varied she had so far undertaken in Canada. Even though the age of television had arrived, crowds everywhere were large. The media itself admitted that the Queen's perform-

Elizabeth II in 1959 became the second Sovereign of Canada to receive the Hudson's Bay Company tribute in person. W.J. Keswick, Governor of the Company, offers the beaver skin, part of the symbolic rent exacted under the Royal Charter granted in 1670 by the Queen's ancestor King Charles II.

With her Canadian Cabinet at Government House, Halifax, before leaving for London. The photograph was taken following the Cabinet meeting at which the Queen gave her approval to the appointment of Major-General Georges Vanier as Governor-General of Canada.

Today the St Lawrence Seaway is taken for granted. That is because it was such a success, fully justifying its construction, and came to have a major economic impact on the two countries that built it. It was the Seaway that permitted the successful exploitation of iron ore in Quebec and Labrador and allowed steel, petroleum products, chemicals, lumber and general goods to be moved through it. In the late 1990's, fifty million tons of cargo a year were being transported via the Seaway compared with eleven million going through the water network in the early '50's. The Queen could be proud of being associated with such a successful Canadian endeavour.

By 1959 Her Majesty had known Canada for almost a decade. She had witnessed its steady growth and development. The population had increased by four million to eighteen million.

Urbanisation had enhanced the importance of Canadian cities and the strength of rural communities was in decline. Accelerated industrialisation, especially in Quebec, and the new social conditions resulting from all the changes, were preparing the "quiet revolutions" of the '60's for both English and French Canada. Economic development was now organised continentally, a fact that was to bring North American Free Trade in the '90's. Although this trend produced prosperity, and Canadian society had become more conscious of itself, continentalism as always carried an unspoken threat to Canadian independence and identity. With the loosening of the Commonwealth, that counterbalance to United States cultural and economic influence, the Monarchy would be more important than ever in preserving Canada. It could do so if allowed to carry out its role and develop

The Queen's new baby, Prince Andrew, 1960.

naturally. The frequent presence of the Queen and the new technology rendered the great royal tours of the century since 1860 obsolete. The 1959 tour was the last of them. In one way this was a pity. Tours that embraced the whole country gave the Queen the maximum opportunity of engendering a sense of community nationally which was one of her main roles. She could still do so on a regional basis but something was lost in the change.

The Queen entered the '60's with a new baby. Prince Andrew, her third child, was born at Buckingham Palace on 19 February 1960. Given the name Andrew after his paternal grandfather Prince Andrew of Greece, the new Prince provided a chance for the Queen to undo in part the slight to her husband of April 1952 when the decision was made about the name of the Royal Family. A few days before giving birth she declared to the United Kingdom Privy Council her wish that some of her descendants use the name Mountbatten-

Windsor. This was a happy year for her family. She had the satisfaction of seeing her sister Princess Margaret married in a splendid ceremony at Westminster Abbey to Anthony Armstrong-Jones, created Earl of Snowdon before the wedding, whom the Princess had met in 1958.

A major crisis left the Queen in no doubt that a new decade had dawned. It proved a watershed for the Commonwealth. Increasing unease had been felt by member countries over the apartheid policy of South Africa's Afrikaans-dominated Government. In May 1960 South Africa made known its intention of abolishing the Monarchy and replacing the Queen with a president. It had every right to do so but the process meant it had to seek readmission to the Commonwealth as a republic. John Diefenbaker, the Queen's Canadian Prime Minister opposed giving South Africa the assurance it demanded in advance that it would be readmitted. Diefenbaker was a strong believer in racial equality and an opponent of apartheid. He knew that many other member states would oppose South Africa continuing to belong to the Commonwealth family. In the South African referendum held on 5 October 1960, the republican side won a slim majority. None of the country's millions of Blacks were of course allowed to vote on the question. Anticipating a rebuff, South Africa withdrew its request to remain a member of the Commonwealth before the actual introduction of the republic on 31 May 1961.

A vote along racial lines would have destroyed the unique world community of nations. Now it was able to continue its championship of racial harmony. Though some of the white member states such as Australia and New Zealand were taken aback at the unexpected confrontation, Diefenbaker's position was the right one to ensure the organisation had a future. South Africa's desire to become a republic was itself a kind of admission that the Monarchy of Elizabeth II and racism were incompatible. The Royal family record on the question of race was a pretty good one. The Queen's ancestress Queen Victoria was noted for her complete lack of racial feeling. (The second Canadian to whom she awarded a Victoria Cross was a Nova Scotia Black named William Hall—at a time when American Blacks were still slaves.) King Edward VII as Prince of Wales and King George V both returned from stays in India appalled at the racism of the Raj. The Queen herself experienced South African racism first hand in 1947 when she saw her father King George VI prevented by the South African Government from shaking hands with the Blacks to whom he presented war medals.

In 1959 Grace Wheatley, a United Kingdom artist, painted an allegory entitled *The Crown* for a London theatre. It shows Elizabeth II in a Garden of Eden-like setting, wearing the Imperial State Crown, Coronation dress and purple mantle, reaching out with her right hand, an Eastern umbrella above her head. Surrounding the Queen are figures representing the peoples of the Commonwealth as well as indigenous animals, birds, flora and fauna. The canvas is a magical vision of colour, grace and harmony. Nothing could better express how the Queen saw her role as Monarch and Head of the Com-

The Crown, an allegorical painting by Grace Wheatley, 1959.

monwealth. Her Majesty in fact had already created a stir by having a black Nigerian equerry at Buckingham Palace for a few weeks prior to her 1956 visit to Nigeria.

In April 1960 the Queen welcomed the French President General Charles de Gaulle to London. The testy French leader, charmed by Her Majesty's French, took the occasion to express his thanks for the support King George VI had given him as leader of the Free French in World War II. "Where else, Madame, better than in your presence could I bear witness to my gratitude?" he said in his speech. On her state visit to Italy in May 1961, the Queen

117

In April 1960 General de Gaulle, the French President, paid a state visit to the Queen in London, her first public engagement since the birth of her third child.

wore the maple leaf dress from 1957 in Canada. The allusion was obvious. Elizabeth II was the Queen not just of the United Kingdom but also of Canada where there was a thriving and rapidly increasing Italian-Canadian community and maples leaves reminded the people of Italy of this other link she had with them. A crowd of 100,000 cheered Her Majesty in Naples and in Rome the Queen had a meeting with the new Pope, John XXIII who had just summoned an Ecumenical Council..

Two major Commonwealth tours took the Queen to Asia and Africa the same year. She was the first Monarch of her line to visit India since King George V's Durbar in 1911. From India she travelled to Pakistan and then to Nepal. The second tour found the Queen a player in the Cold War which was heating up and for which the whole world had become the battlefield. A visit to Ghana had been postponed in 1960 because of the Queen's

pregnancy. The Soviet Union was wooing Kwame Nkrumah, President of the new state of Ghana, independent since 1957, a republic since 1960, and there was fear that Ghana would be lost to the Commonwealth and the Free World. Nkrumah very much wanted a visit from the Queen who was eager to go given the stakes. But violence in the country, especially its capital Accra, where supporters of the opposition (imprisoned by Nkrumah) were attempting to kill the President, raised fears for the Queen's safety and led to demands that the visit be cancelled. The Queen insisted on going. "How silly I should look" she said, "if I was scared to visit Ghana and then Khrushchev [the Soviet leader] went and had a good reception". She did go and the visit was a triumph. A journalist described the Queen as "the best protection Nkrumah had had for years". Her Majesty returned to London in safety, Nkrumah soon went the way of all dictators.

With Pope John XXIII at the Vatican, 1961.

Riding an elephant on her way to a Durbar in Jaipur, India, January 1961.

The Queen marked the latest advance in communications when she opened a new eighty-circuit trans-Atlantic telephone cable on 18 December 1961. Newspaper pictures showed her smiling happily, holding the telephone as she spoke from Buckingham Palace to John Diefenbaker, the Canadian Prime Minister,

in Ottawa. Not all her Canadian news was good that year however. Earlier the Queen expressed her sorrow to provincial authorities over the destruction of a million-and-a-half acres of timber in Newfoundland by forest fires.

The newest addition to the distinct features of the Canadian Monarchy appeared in 1962. On the advice of the Canadian Government and at her own suggestion, the Queen adopted a personal Canadian flag by Royal Warrant. The frequent presence of the Queen in the country now

Personal flag adopted by the Queen as Queen of Canada 1962.

made such a flag a necessity. The banner consisted of Her Majesty's Royal Arms of Canada in the middle of which was her person cypher, a crowned E in gold, at the centre of a dark blue circle surrounded by gold roses. The inspiration for the flag came from the personal one that had been adopted at the Queen's own instigation for Sierra Leone the previous year. The Queen's flag was to be used in whatever place in the country the Sovereign was personally present. The '60's were to see a host of new flags adopted in Canada, provincially and nationally. It can be said the Queen got in ahead of them all.

The tour of Ghana was fraught with danger. By her triumph there the Queen struck a blow for the Free World and the Commonwealth.

COMMEMORATING THE QUEEN'S LIFE

One of the ways in which Canadians and citizens of the Commonwealth remember historic royal events is through the collection of royal commemoratives. The highlights of the Queen's life have been recalled in this way for over seven decades.

A "Two for Joy" Paragon tea service produced in 1926 to mark the birth of Princess Elizabeth.

A Paragon cup and saucer celebrates a young Elizabeth as "Our Empire's Little Princess" based on a Marcus Adams' photograph.

A Manitoba school commemoration of the Coronation of King George VI in 1937 featured Princess Elizabeth in the top right corner.

Princess Elizabeth and Princess Margaret are depicted on this commemorative of the 1939 Royal Tour of Canada, although they did not accompany their parents.

A Paragon china pin dish and a plate by Cassadian celebrated the 1951 tour of Canada by Princess Elizabeth and the Duke of Edinburgh.

With the Queen's Accession commemoratives flourished, such as a 1953 Royal Doulton loving cup of the Queen on horseback, one of the "Courage" designs. It proclaims "Here's a health unto Her Majesty".

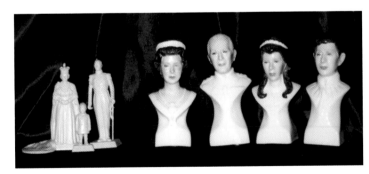

Plastic Coronation figurines of the Queen, Duke and Prince Charles are depicted on the left. The Crown Staffordshire busts of the Queen, Duke, Princess Anne and Prince Charles are from a later period.

The Royal Family are commemorated in this Salisbury cup and saucer and Royal Standard dish.

The Ontario Official Royal Map of 1953 also commemorated the Queen's Coronation.

Royal visits are often marked with inexpensive pins for people to wear, as in the 1959 and 1984 examples shown.

A group of pieces made for the 1959 opening of the St Lawrence Seaway—mug, plate, tea cup and candy dish.

HI THERE !!

A homemade Christmas card from the early 1960's with the Queen is an example of an amateur but popular expression of royal commemoration.

An Alfred Meakin pottery plate also celebrated the 1959 tour. It depicts the BRITANNIA, the Queen, Duke of Edinburgh and Dwight Eisenhower, and the Great Lakes—St Lawrence waterway. Only a few Canadian souvenirs showed the President and the American part of the Seaway.

Another, this time commercial, 1960's commemorative was a Vancouver manufactured jigsaw puzzle card of the Queen.

A 1982 plate marked the patriation of the Canadian Constitution by Her Majesty the Queen. It displays, in addition to Her Majesty, the Canadian National and Canadian Royal Union Flags, the Royal Fleur de Lys Shield of Canadian history and the Canadian royal badge of three maple leaves, as well as the Royal Arms of the Provinces.

The Queen's 1984 tour of Canada was marked by a pair of mugs depicting the Queen and Duke of Edinburgh respectively on the front of each and the Crown on the back.

A Coalport tea cup and saucer and an Aynsley mug celebrated the 60th birthday of the Queen.

A hand bag depicting the Crown, aboriginal drums and a map of northwestern Canada commemorated the 1994 royal tour of the west.

A special postcard also marked the 1994 tour.

In 1992 the Queen unveiled the statue of herself on Parliament Hill in Ottawa. This t-shirt was marketed to celebrate the event. The Roman numerals give the date—30 June 1992.

6

"The Wind of Change"

1964–1976

When the year 1964 began, the world was in transition. The United States had lost its president the previous fall to an assassin's bullet in Dallas. That president had already begun American involvement in the quagmire of Vietnam. His successor would instigate an incident in the Gulf of Tonkin before the year was out that would thrust the United States into a massive commit-ment and the longest war in its history. The war, which would be the first the Americans would lose since the War of 1812 against Canada, fostered a massive student protest movement against the conflict and the accepted values of the United States generally. At the same time the civil rights movement was also sweeping American society and tackling racial issues that had been buried from public view for

In 1985 the Queen posed with the British Prime Ministers of her reign, including, from the left, James Callaghan, Lord Home (Alec Home), Margaret Thatcher, Lord Stockton (Harold Macmillan), Lord Wilson (Harold Wilson) and Edward Heath. All except Mrs Thatcher had played a role in the tumultuous years from 1964 to 1976.

generations. Together the two movements would shake the United States to its foundations and influence young people throughout the world.

The Soviet Union, feeling humiliated after the 1962 Cuban Missile Crisis which almost led to World War III, had already embarked on creating a naval fleet and expanding its military strength to challenge the Americans. It was a futile effort as the Americans, even though weakened by Vietnam and internal self-doubt, could still outspend any competitor. The ultimate result for the Soviet Union was bankruptcy—economic and political—and the end of the communist state itself in 1989.

So it was all around the world in the "Swinging Sixties" or the revolutionary sixties. China was wracked by the Cultural Revolution launched by the tyrant Mao Zedong against his own people. The Afrikaaners of South Africa, having left the Commonwealth in 1961 when they abolished their monarchical government for a republican regime based on apartheid, were sowing the seeds of a generation-long civil war and their own destruction. Cuba, under its dictator Fidel Castro, was gearing up to be the home of international communist terrorism for Latin America and eventually even Africa. In the Middle East, Israel and her Arab neighbours were taking a brief respite before beginning a new round of wars and insurrections. Within a few years it would seem as if revolution was everywhere in the world.

In the social world the slogan among many of the young was "turn on and drop out". The Beatles would arrive in New York in 1964 and popular music would change dramatically. The drug culture and the sexual revolution were to follow. On the other hand a technological revolution was underway and scientists were getting high in a different sense as they reached for the moon and beyond. Likewise the Second Vatican Council was meeting and would transform the Roman Catholic Church.

In such an age, when the cry "don't trust anyone over thirty" was heard, what chance did an institution like the Crown have, which was thirty times thirty years old? Even the incumbent monarch, Elizabeth II, was now 37, once considered young but over that imaginary threshold.

Among the realms of Queen Elizabeth II, the United Kingdom began to withdraw from Empire completely and at an accelerated rate, bending to what Sir Harold Macmillan, the former prime minister, had called "the wind of change". Britain was also starting on its rocky path leading eventually in 1973 to membership in the European Union, then called simply the Common Market. Although this had little immediate impact on the other realms in the 1960s, it was to prove a major step in fostering republican movements in Australia and New Zealand in later decades. Membership in the Union would mean, as its critics feared, turning away economically (and eventually politically and culturally) from the Commonwealth.

Anthony Sampson, the biographer of Macmillan, wrote that "The negotiations [started by Macmillan to join the Common Market] and the new climate they produced, turned Britain more firmly toward Europe; and the Commonwealth never loomed so large again". In her Christmas Message of 1972, when

Britain's admission had been approved and was to take effect the next year, the Queen addressed these concerns. Her Majesty said "The new links with Europe will not replace those with the Commonwealth. They cannot alter our historical and personal attachments with kinsmen and friends overseas. Old friends will not be lost. Britain will take her Commonwealth links into Europe with her."

In fact, despite the Queen's wishes, it was not to be the reality. In hindsight it can be seen that after the British decision to join Europe, beginning in the sixties and culminating in 1973, the strength of the Crown in the Queen's realms could no longer rely on the Commonwealth link as a major pillar. From then on, if it was not already the case, the Queen's role in each country would depend on the internal heritage and commitment to monarchy. In other words, each of the Queen's monarchies would stand or fall on its own, and the Queen would not have one battle to fight but many separate ones.

This change had the greatest impact on the Antipodes, where the Crown was associated with British ties to a greater extent than in Canada, where nationalism and the "Canadian Crown" were perhaps older concepts.

In Britain, while there was the usual carping about the Queen's accent and old-fashioned ways and calls for changes, the Monarchy itself seemed secure. The major challenge the Queen faced in the United Kingdom in constitutional terms was the role of the monarch in selecting the prime minister in the more democratic world of the late twentieth century. In October 1963 Sir Harold Macmillan took ill and sud-denly decided to retire. Unlike the British Labour Party and the political parties in Canada and other parts of the Commonwealth, the British Conservative Party had no set procedure, such as a convention, for choosing a new leader. Instead a leader was expected to "emerge" through consensus and, when the party was in power, the monarch would have the authority to appoint that person as Prime Minister. No one knew for sure, but the public believed that Rab Butler was preferred by the party rank and file, Lord Hailsham by the Conservative M.P.s and Alec Home by Macmillan and the Cabinet. It was the Queen's prerogative to choose her Prime Minister, but there was disquiet and criticism as to the methods she was able to use in ascertaining who was the preferred leader, in making that choice. In the end she chose Home.

The next year, 1964, Home's Conservatives were defeated by the Labour Party of Harold Wilson, who was appointed Prime Minister by the Queen. Shortly after, Home himself introduced an election procedure in the Conservative Party for choosing a leader. 1964 thus marked a fundamental change in Britain, not in the constitutional exercise of the Queen's prerogative but in the practical use of her authority in doing so, as she would generally only have to determine in future which party had the support of the Commons rather than which individual had the support of his or her party.

The other development in Britain that the Queen had to deal with concerned finances. By the 1970s inflation meant that the Civil List was insufficient to meet the costs of the Crown. In 1971 Parliament was asked to increase the list and, while this was approved, it was the

The Queen is flanked by her heir, the Prince of Wales, and her husband, the Duke of Edinburgh, at the 1969 investiture of the Prince of Wales in Caernarvan Castle.

beginning of the constant questioning of the "cost of the monarchy" and whether the taxpayer was getting "value for money". The argument that the Civil List was not a salary for the Queen or other members of the Royal Family but paid for the administrative expenses they faced, or the fact that the funds were not drawn from general revenue raised from taxpayers but from the revenues of the Crown Lands was quickly lost to demagoguery and the tabloid press. It is an issue which has never since gone away and, like the proverbial genie let out of

the bottle, does not seem likely to be put back in.

In the Royal Family's personal life there were a number of changes and innovations. On 10 March 1964 a fourth child and third son was born to the Queen—Prince Edward—thus completing her family. In 1972 the Queen and Duke of Edinburgh celebrated the silver jubilee of their wedding and the next year the Queen's only daughter, Princess Anne became the first of her children to marry, when she wed Captain Mark Phillips. The two had met in equestrian competitions where they rode for the British National team. The Princess had followed her mother's example in developing a love for horses and was an expert horsewoman. She acquired her first horse after leaving school in 1968 and by 1976 she was competing in the Olympic Games for the British team.

On 1 July 1969, Prince Charles, who had been created Prince of Wales in 1958, was formally invested with the title at a ceremony in Caernarvon Castle which combined traditional ceremony and modern design, arranged by his uncle Lord Snowdon, husband of Princess Margaret. Nationalism was rearing its head in the United Kingdom itself as well as around the Commonwealth and there were threats by Welsh separatists of hoax bombs and real bombs. Prior to his investiture the Prince attended classes for a term at the University College of Wales in Aberystwyth where he learnt Welsh. This followed his earlier pre-university schooling at Gourdonston in Scotland and Geelong Grammar School in Australia.

Following upon the success of these experiments with the Prince of Wales, in 1976 Prince Andrew was sent to school at Lakefield College in Ontario, Canada. If anything this proved even more successful than the experiment with Prince Charles. Prince Andrew developed a close relationship with Canada and Canadians that has grown ever since.

Two television experiments were also launched in the 1960s. In 1966 a show entitled *The Royal Palaces of Britain* was produced by the BBC and ITV. Created by Sir Kenneth Clark (later Lord Clark), it explored Buckingham Palace, Windsor Castle, Kensington Palace, St James's Palace, Hampton Court, and Holyroodhouse Palace. It paved the way for the even more ambitious *The Royal Family* in 1969, which presented viewers with an inside look at the life of the Royal Family at work and in private. It was a tremendous success, viewed by a larger worldwide audience than any documentary until that time. It gave the Queen's subjects and the larger world a sense of closeness to her that they had not had before. On the other hand it was thought by some at the time, and many more subsequently, that it let in too much "daylight upon the magic" beginning the media coverage that became the media intrusiveness

The Silver Wedding anniversary of the Queen and Prince Philip was marked throughout the Commonwealth in 1972. First day cover from the Turks and Caicos Islands

of later decades and has plagued the Royal Family ever since and exacerbated, if it did not actually create, many of the personal and institutional problems they have faced.

In the constitutional and political sphere, one significant change for the Queen arose in

Informal photograph of the Queen in 1975 by Peter Grugeon.

Africa, Asia and the West Indies, as part of the decolonising process. Marxism as well as nationalism was fashionable in the "Third World" and in the "First World" universities which trained "First" and "Third World" leaders. While nationalism might embrace monarchy, Marxism was inherently hostile to it. The Crown had to deal with both. In this environment the newly created countries had to decide whether to become independent monarchies under the Queen or another monarch, or republics.

There was also the effect on the Commonwealth as the association grew in numbers. By 1964 there were twenty-two countries. Five were monarchies under the Queen. One was a

monarchy with a different monarch. Sixteen were republics. Between 1964 and 1977 twenty new members were added to the Commonwealth as they became independent. Six of these became monarchies under the Queen: Barbados (1966), Mauritius (1968), Fiji (1970), The Bahamas (1973), Grenada (1974) and Papua New Guinea (1975). Mauritius and Fiji however subsequently became republics. Four more became monarchies with separate monarchs. These were Lesotho (1966), Swaziland (1968), Tonga (1970) and Western Samoa (1970). Finally there were ten which became republics: Malawi (1964), Malta (1964), Zambia (1964), Singapore (1965), The Gambia (1965), Botswana (1966), Guyana (1966), Nauru (1968), Bangladesh (1972) and Seychelles (1976).

That left the total at the time of Her Majesty's Silver Jubilee at forty-two countries—eleven monarchies under the Queen, five other monarchies and twenty-six republics. In addition Rhodesia declared unilateral independence in 1965, when the white dominated government of Ian Smith preferred a republic to sharing power with the majority black population. The percentage of monarchies under the Queen actually went up in this period from 22% of the Commonwealth to 25%. This perhaps demonstrated the affection and loyalty in which the Queen was held and the resilience of the Crown in the non-white areas of the Commonwealth, from which the Queen drew strength and to which she added strength. The Queen was now separately Queen of far more countries than any of her predecessors had ever been.

How the Commonwealth would deal with

South Africa and Rhodesia remained a constant issue at heads of government meetings, often, but not always, with a division on tactics, if not strategy, between the old "white" nations and the newer ones. Canada usually sided with the newer countries however, and while the Queen never stated a political preference on matters, such as sanctions against South Africa, which divided her peoples, she was certainly considered a friend of the black majorities in these troubled lands. In 1965 she wrote a letter to Ian Smith, trying unsuccessfully to head off the unilateral declaration of independence.

The Queen undertook many tours of the "New Commonwealth". The Caribbean saw her in February and March of 1966, Malta in November 1967, Fiji and Tonga in 1970, Singapore, Malaysia, Brunei, the Maldive Islands, the Seychelles, Mauritius and Kenya in February and March 1972, the Solomon Islands and Papua New Guinea in 1974, Barbados, the Bahamas and Bermuda in February 1975, Jamaica in April that year for the Commonwealth Conference and Hong Kong in May.

Foreign lands were also the scene of state visits by the Queen: Ethiopia, Sudan and West Germany in 1965, Belgium in 1966, France in 1967, Brazil, Chile and Senegal in 1968, Austria and Norway in 1969, Turkey in 1971, Thailand, France and Yugoslavia in 1972, Indonesia in 1974, Mexico and Japan in 1975, and Finland, the United States and Luxembourg in 1976.

The years from 1964 until the Queen's Silver Jubilee proved relatively quiet in Australia and New Zealand—that is until 1975. Her Majesty did not visit either country between 1963 and 1970, then undertook a two-month trip from March 1970 until 5 May to both countries. This trip was to mark the bicentenary of Captain Cook's voyage of discovery in the Pacific. She was accompanied by the Duke of Edinburgh and, for part of the trip, by the Prince of Wales and Princess Anne. It was

The Queen and the Japanese Emperor, Hirohito exchange toasts at a dinner in Tokyo in 1975. The Queen not only travelled throughout the Commonwealth but around the world.

on this trip that the Queen introduced the first modern "walkabout". New Zealanders coined the term to describe the Queen walking among her ordinary subjects, not just speaking to those invited to organised venues. The Queen's

In 1976 the Queen visited the United States for that country's bicentenary. She was entertained by the American President, Gerald Ford at a state dinner.

mother, Queen Elizabeth, the Consort of King George VI, had in fact invented the walkabout in Ottawa in 1939 when she spontaneously went into a crowd of veterans with the King to speak to them, and pre-Victorian monarchs had also walked on the streets among the people. But after New Zealand in 1970 the action and the term became a regular feature of all royal tours.

In October 1973 the Queen was back in Australia to open the Sydney Opera House and in January and February 1974 the Queen and Duke undertook another extensive tour of the area, including the Cook Islands, Norfolk Island, New Hebrides, British Solomon Islands and Papua New Guinea as well as New Zealand, where she attended the Commonwealth Games, and Australia, where she opened the Australian Parliament.

Then in 1975 a constitutional crisis emerged in Australia which involved the Crown. In the Australian Parliament both the upper house (the Senate) and the lower house (the House of Representatives) are elected by the people, and both are required to pass money bills. (In the United Kingdom and Canada the House of Lords and the Senate also pass money bills, but because the houses are hereditary and appointed, it is constitutional convention that they cannot reject or amend them.) The Labour government of Gough Whitlam had a majority in the lower house but the opposition controlled

Australian portrait of the Queen in 1955 by Sir William Dargie, featured Her Majesty dressed in the colours of Australia and wearing the wattle flower, the national emblem of the country, on her shoulder. Prints of the painting were distributed by the Monarchist League in Australia to illustrate the Queen's Australian identity as republican rumblings began in the Antipodes in the middle of the 1970s.

the upper house and rejected the government's budget. The Prime Minister then asked the Governor-General, Sir John Kerr, who had been appointed by the Queen on the recommendation of Mr Whitlam, to dissolve only the Senate and call for new Senate elections. Sir John, quite correctly, rejected this odd suggestion and replied that he would dissolve both houses if requested for a general election to let the people decide, or the government would have to negotiate with the Senate to get a budget passed to carry on governing. Mr Whitlam refused the first and could not achieve the second. The Governor-General dismissed him, since he could not govern without a budget, and appointed opposition leader Malcolm Fraser as Prime Minister on condition he request a general election. This happened and the Australian people returned the Liberal—National coalition of Mr Fraser with a majority in both houses.

While the crisis had nothing to do with colonialism but was an example of the Australian Monarchy working as it was intended to do, to ensure that the people had the government they wished, the republican Gough Whitlam used the crisis shamelessly to whip up sentiment against the Crown and imaginary British imperialism, and misled many into believing the Governor-General had acted to subvert democracy rather than facilitate it. As this incident followed the admission two years earlier of the United Kingdom into the European Common Market, it proved a potent force against the Crown. Demonstrations greeted the Queen on her Silver Jubilee tour in 1977 and an active republican movement gained strength, despite the obvious fact that a president would

probably have acted exactly the same as the Governor-General did.

The Crown of course had to remain non-partisan, despite the fact that it was being attacked, and rely on its supporters to defend it. What had once been considered the most loyal part of the "Old Commonwealth" was now beginning to feel the wind of change and it was an ill wind. It had not blown as far as New Zealand however.

The major challenge to the Queen's sovereignty in the 1960s and 1970s came, however, in Canada, the oldest of the dominions and the first of the "Old Commonwealth" to truly face "the wind of change".

Neither Canadian nor Quebec nationalism began in 1964. Their roots went far deeper. But 1964 changed, or at least conveyed the change, that has characterised the past four decades in the country. It was undoubtedly a watershed. The "Quiet Revolution" was the designation given to Quebec's peaceful change from a Catholic, conservative society to a secular, liberal one after the end of Maurice Duplessis's years as Premier in 1959. This was either seen as good or bad depending on the observer's perspective. What was not noted at the time, perhaps, was that a similar quiet revolution was taking place in English Canada. It was not from a conservative to a liberal society, both held significant sway, but it involved the same questioning of traditional institutions and was characterised by increased continentalism, or Americanisation. The Crown had always been a bulwark against continentalism.

The years 1964 to 1976 in Canada were the years of centennial celebrations and each generated a tour by the Queen. 1964 itself marked the centenaries of the Charlottetown Conference and the Quebec Conference. It was in Charlottetown, the capital of Prince Edward Island, that the Fathers of Canadian Confederation first decided to unite the British North American provinces into one country. This was confirmed and the details largely finalised at the Quebec Conference later that year, which led to the creation of the Dominion of Canada in 1867. 1967, of course, marked the one hundredth anniversary of Canada and was known as Centennial Year. Manitoba joined in 1870. The Northwest Territories (modern day Saskatchewan, Alberta, Northwest Territories, Yukon Territory and Nunavut Territory) were created that same year out of land transferred by the British Crown and sold by the Hudson's Bay Company to the Canadian Crown. British Columbia was the next to join Canada, in 1871. Ironically, Prince Edward Island, the "birthplace of Confederation" did not join Canada until 1873. While Ontario, Quebec, Nova Scotia and New Brunswick celebrated their centenaries as provinces of Canada in 1967, three provinces and the Northwest Territories celebrated in 1970, 1971 and 1973. The Queen was in Canada for each of the anniversaries. She also came to Canada in 1976 for the first Olympic Games to be held in the country.

The 1964 Canadian royal tour began on a positive note among enthusiastic crowds in Prince Edward Island.

THE QUEEN'S CANADIAN FIRST MINISTERS

Nine Canadians have served Her Majesty as her Canadian Prime Minister (literally "first servant") since she became Queen of Canada in 1952. They are (clockwise) Louis St Laurent (1952–1957), John Diefenbaker (1957–1963), Lester Pearson (1963–1968), Pierre Trudeau (1968–1979 & 1980–1984); next page, Joe Clark (1979–1980), John Turner (1984, not shown), Brian Mulroney (1984–1993), Kim Campbell (1993, not shown) and Jean Chretién (1993–present).

In 1976 the Queen and Duke of Edinburgh posed on the deck of the BRITANNIA with all of Her Majesty's representatives (Governor-General and Provincial Lieutenant-Governors) and first ministers (Prime Minister and Provincial Premiers).

The centenaries galvanised the new nationalism in Canada, a sentiment strengthened by the Queen's proclamation of a national flag for the country in February 1965, after a rancorous debate in 1964, for part of which the Queen was in Canada. The "Maple Leaf Flag", as it was known, replaced the Canadian Red Ensign which had been used in one variation or another (as the Canadian Shield changed), since Confederation. The Ensign was not considered Canadian enough by some nationalists because it had the "British" Union Flag in the corner. As part of this national mood the Queen was later advised by the Canadian government to establish the Order of Canada in 1967 as the first order in a distinctively Canadian honours system.

There was a split in the new nationalism. While most Canadian nationalists remained loyal to the Crown as the embodiment of a modern Canadian identity in a republican continent, as it had been for the older Canada, others believed that the Canadian Monarchy was too "British" because the Queen of Canada lived in London most of the time. They advocated a republic with a "Canadian" head of state. These republican nationalists, usually non-French Canadians, also maintained that French Canada desired a Canadian republic. Events were to show that French-Canadian republicans in fact desired a Quebec republic, not a Canadian one, and the old fear that republicanism in any form meant Americanisation was still real.

In French Canada meanwhile there was a growing parallel Quebec nationalism. While most believed it was possible to realise this nationalism within Canada—"*maître chez nous*" ("masters in our own house") was the slogan—a growing number were suggesting that if Canada could only thrive by being non-British, perhaps it was also true that Quebec could only thrive by being non-Canadian. The Quiet Revolution, launched by the provincial Liberals under Jean Lesage at the beginning of the sixties was neither anti-Canadian nor anti-monarchical but, like all the revolutions of the sixties, it fostered an atmosphere where institutions were questioned. In Quebec this included the Church, the Crown, the role of government, the primacy of English, and Canada itself.

The "night of the batons" in Montreal.

Another development in Canada that was to call the Monarchy into question was the large number of non-British, non-French and non-European immigrants who came in these years. Canada had always been a multicultural country but by the 1970s it became more so. Multiculturalism received official recognition as government policy when the initial sixties' idea of "bilingualism and biculturalism" became "bilingualism and multiculturalism" in the seventies. "How could such non-British people relate to the Monarchy?", republicans asked, ignoring the fact that many, if not most, had come from other parts of the Commonwealth, and that monarchy was not a uniquely British idea in any case.

These were the attitudes that had emerged or were beginning to emerge as the Queen set out on a tour of Canada in October 1964. It was to be far different from her three previous trips. The 1964 tour began peacefully and happily enough in Prince Edward Island, though tension was in the air because of these growing ideas and because Quebec separatists had threatened violence when the tour reached that province. The demonstrations took place and they got out of hand. The police, unused to dealing with such a situation, over-reacted. The worst evening was known as the "night of the batons" in Montreal and many police and demonstrators were injured while the Queen carried out her programme of events. Canadians had not seen such a sight in decades, and never in connection with a royal tour, and it shocked them. To some it was proof that the Monarchy was a source of division in the country and should be sacrificed to satisfy Quebec nationalism.

Others were wiser and did not blame the Crown, which they realised was a target because it was convenient and because it was a symbol of Canadian unity, which the separatists opposed, not disunity. Jean Lesage, the Premier of the province, was so moved by the Queen's calmness and courage in the face of the violence that he kept breaking into tears. The Queen

The Queen spoke from the Throne in the Legislative Council chamber of the Quebec Provincial Parliament.

The Queen cuts the cake celebrating 100 years of Canadian Confederation on Parliament Hill in Ottawa, 1 July 1967.

herself stated emphatically in French to the Quebec Legislative Assembly "I am pleased to think that there exists in our Commonwealth a country where I can express myself officially in French."

The French language publication, *L'Action*, was more aware of the history of Quebec than many self-proclaimed Quebec or Canadian nationalists. Following the incidents of the tour it emphatically asserted: "Long before Ottawa was seized, as it is now, of the bilingual and bicultural ferment, the Crown was establishing the fact, in all its interventions in Canada, of equality of the two languages beyond the letter

of the Constitution. The Queen as an ally of Quebec nationalism? And why not? In a sense she always has been."

As *L'Action* understood, and historically most Canadians had believed, the Crown had always stood for a positive Canadian nationalism, which was rooted in its heritage, respectful of the country's diversity, especially its French character, and dedicated to a distinctive Canadian identity in North America.

But it was now clear that this had been forgotten, or was being conveniently hidden by many. The challenge in the years ahead for the Queen, which she readily accepted, was to reassert the historic roles of Canada's royal identity in the changed conditions of the late twentieth century—fostering Canadian independence, diversity and unity. While her supporters regretted that it was even necessary to restate and defend the obvious, it was evident the contest would have to be joined openly and clearly by Her Majesty if her Canadian Crown were to survive and thrive. The Queen's speeches to Canadians over the next decade reflected that undertaking.

In 1967 the Queen presided as Queen of Canada over the centennial celebration in Ottawa and visited the site of Expo '67 in Montreal, where Canada showed its best side to the world and invited the world to visit. In Ottawa the Queen said "It is these, the ordinary people of Canada, who have given flesh and sinew to the plans of the Fathers of Confederation."

In 1970 the government of Pierre Trudeau, who was not noted for his monarchical sympathies and who had speculated in 1968 that the Canadian Monarchy would end within a

At Expo '67 in Montreal the Queen rides the popular minirail.

eignty through the presence of the Canadian Sovereign. And the point was made. The Queen was accompanied not only by the Duke of Edinburgh but also by the Prince of Wales and Princess Anne. The Queen also used the opportunity of this tour to reiterate the need and tradition of Canadians to work together, despite their differences. She returned to the theme in two notable speeches.

"I count myself fortunate to be at the head of a state in which such a society [open to everyone] exists and which is strongly established in freedom and tolerance", she said in Winnipeg. At Yellowknife she said that "In this modern world we hear all too much about the enmities and quarrels between men of different races and religions. I hope that you will always remember that, except for the great commercial rivalries between the companies in the days of the fur trade, French, English and Scots, Indians,

decade, found a new need for the Crown when the traditional challenge to Canadian sovereignty came, as it had always come, not from London but from Washington. The American government questioned Canadian sovereignty over the north. Mr Trudeau knew that the best way to get international attention for Canada's determination not to give way on the question, was to have the Queen of Canada visit the Arctic. The Governor-General or even he himself, as Prime Minister, would attract little attention for the Canadian position internationally, where it was needed.

And so, coincident with celebrating the centenary of Manitoba and the Northwest Territories in 1970, the Queen's tour of the Arctic was a direct government statement of Canadian sover-

In 1970 the Queen travelled to the Arctic to assert Canadian sovereignty.

141

While accompanying the Queen on her 1971 visit to British Columbia, Princess Anne, watched by Her Majesty, laid the cornerstone for the Canadian Broadcasting Corporation's regional headquarters in the province. The children of the Queen began taking a more active role in the "family firm" in the 1970s.

Eskimos and Métis, all worked and lived together in a difficult and dangerous environment. They faced the rigours of a harsh climate and natural obstacles of a new land and under those testing conditions only the true value of the individual had any importance. This is a lesson we should always remember."

British Columbia was the locale for the Queen's tour of 1971 and at a citizenship ceremony in Vancouver she told a group of her new Canadian subjects that "Canadian unity is not uniformity." On that trip she also reminded Canadians that what she had dedicated her life to was a good standard for all: "We hear altogether too much about struggles for power these days. I believe we should be more concerned with giving service."

The year 1973 brought the Queen to Prince Edward Island again to mark its centenary and she also visited Ontario, Saskatchewan and Alberta. In Toronto, Ontario, the metropolis of Canada, and quickly becoming the most multicultural city in the most multicultural province, the Queen reached out again to new Canadians, to demonstrate that the legacy of the Crown in Canada, which may not have been their birthright, was their right by adoption. "I want the Crown to be seen as a symbol of national sovereignty belonging to all," Her Majesty declared, "It is not only a link between Commonwealth nations, but between Canadian citizens of every national origin and ancestry."

She elaborated on that same trip on how they could embrace the Crown and Canadian heritage: "Canada asks no citizens to deny their forebears, to forsake their inheritance—only that each should accept and value the cultural freedom of others as he enjoys his own. It is a gentle invitation, this call to citizenship and I urge those who have accepted the invitation to participate fully in the building of the Canadian society and to demonstrate the real meaning of the brotherhood of man."

Pierre Trudeau was noted for being unpredictable, and he surprised everyone by initiating a new role for the Queen in the Commonwealth. In 1972 he invited the Queen to attend the 1973 Commonwealth Heads of Government Conference to be held in Ottawa. These meetings had begun as the old Imperial Conferences in Queen Victoria's reign and were held irregularly at first. By the 1970s they were being held every two or three years, but the Queen had only participated when they took place in London, and not at the first two held outside the United Kingdom.

The Queen readily accepted Mr Trudeau's suggestion, and she has attended every conference since, wherever they are held. This has strengthened her role as Head of the Commonwealth, distinct from being Queen of the United Kingdom, and also highlighted her role as Queen of other countries. In July of 1973 she welcomed the Commonwealth to Ottawa as Queen of Canada and Head of the Commonwealth and not as the British Queen.

The Times of London noted the obvious benefit to Canada of the development: "Trudeau certainly believes that the Commonwealth connection helps Canadians to think globally and not sectionally; and that the Commonwealth, by focusing attention on Ottawa, will help to

"I want the Crown to be seen as a symbol of national sovereignty belonging to all." The Queen speaks to leaders of Toronto's multicultural community at a city hall walkabout in 1973.

preserve a Canadian identity distinct from the United States."

At the same time the schizophrenic nature of the Trudeau government was evident in the ongoing removal of royal symbols and practices in various departments, despite opposition from many Canadians and opinion polls that showed republicanism was only supported by a minority in the country. This was partially tolerated because the Queen was in the country so often for the centenaries that many people did not notice that institutional symbols were disappearing. There was opposition from some cabinet ministers to the Queen opening the 1976 Olympic Games. And the government was busy preparing a constitutional package for Canada that would threaten the Monarchy's very existence when it was introduced in 1978.

But the Queen did open the XXI Olympic Games in Montreal and there were no significant demonstrations or opposition to her presence. Her Majesty also visited the provinces of Nova Scotia, New Brunswick and Ontario on

The Premier of Saskatchewan, Hon. Allan Blakeney, greets Her Majesty on her arrival in the province during her 1973 tour of Canada.

the trip. She was joined by the Duke of Edinburgh, the Prince of Wales, Princess Anne and Capt. Mark Phillips, Prince Andrew and Prince Edward at Bromont, Quebec. It was the first time that the entire immediate Royal Family had been together on Canadian soil.

As the Queen prepared to celebrate the Silver Jubilee of her reign, she could look back on the past dozen years with mixed feelings. In an age when many traditional institutions were under attack and were unable to withstand the assault at all or were greatly weakened, her Crown had been no exception in facing these challenges, but it had fared better than many. Reflecting on his comment about

a "wind of change" in 1960, Sir Harold Macmillan noted even then it was already getting out of hand, "I spoke of a wind of change … but that's not the same thing as a howling tempest".

The Queen had adjusted to the "wind of change" and, when necessary, faced "the howling tempest". In 1947 she had spoken of an "Imperial Commonwealth" but had overseen and embraced its transformation into a Commonwealth of national monarchies and republics. Her contribution and commitment to their success was beyond question. In Canada she was a living example of bilingualism, demonstrated her appeal to the new multicultural society and defended Canada's sovereignty in her role as Queen of Canada. But, despite her efforts, the future of her national monarchies was far from certain as her Silver Jubilee began.

A Canadian first day cover celebrates the 1973 Commonwealth Conference in Ottawa, the first outside of the United Kingdom attended by the Queen.

Despite opposition from some cabinet ministers, the Queen opened the Olympic Games at Montreal in 1976.

The whole Royal Family gathered at Bromont, Quebec during the Olympics. The Queen and Duke of Edinburgh were joined by Princess Anne who was competing in equestrian events, her husband Captain Mark Phillips, the Prince of Wales, Prince Andrew and Prince Edward.

Honours of Her Crown

As Queen of Canada Her Majesty is the fount of all honours. The Canadian honours system consists essentially of three categories — precedence, orders & decorations, and heraldry. Precedence is only conferred upon those who serve the Queen in Canada, such as her representatives, judges, privy counsellors, senators, members of parliament, etc. These individuals hold office and bear prefixes such as Right Honourable or Honourable. Orders and decorations are created by the Queen and granted by her or by her representatives on her behalf. Heraldry in Canada has been administered since 1988 by the Canadian Heraldic Authority, which exercises the heraldic powers of the Queen on Her Majesty's behalf. The Authority is headed by the Queen's Governor-General of Canada as the Queen's heraldic authority in London is administered by the Earl Marshal of England, who prior to 1988 also exercised the Queen's authority in Canada.

Arms of Dominion and Sovereignty of Her Majesty the Queen in Right of Canada, or the Royal Arms of Canada for short, are the Queen's Arms as Queen of Canada. Because they are the Queen's Arms, in 1994 Her Majesty approved their augmentation with the annulus of the Order of Canada around the shield, signifying that the Queen is Sovereign of the Order. Members of the Order similarly encircle their arms with the annulus as well.

Order of Canada, established by the Queen in 1967.

Order of Military Merit of Canada, established by the Queen in 1972.

Victoria Cross, Canada's highest decoration, reconstituted by Her Majesty in 1992.

Obverse of the Cross of Valour, Canada's highest civilian decoration, established by Her Majesty in 1972.

Reverse of the Police Exemplary Service Medal, created by the Queen in 1983.

Gulf and Kuwait War Medal, awarded by the Queen to those who served in the 1991 campaign against Iraq.

Canadian Forces Decoration, bearing the image of the Queen, is the long-service medal for the Canadian Forces. Several members of the Royal Family, including the Queen, the Duke of Edinburgh, the Prince of Wales, the Duke of York, the Princess Royal, the Queen Mother, the Duke of Kent, Princess Alexandra and Countess Mountbatten have received the decoration for their service in the Canadian Forces.

Order of Merit of Saskatchewan, one of the provincial honours, bears the Queen's Crown.

The 1999 grant of arms to the Monarchist League of Canada, approved by Her Majesty the Queen. The Queen's personal approval allowed the use of the Crown by this patriotic organisation.

In 1959 the Queen decorated a Canadian soldier at an investiture in Rideau Hall. This investiture was under the "old" (i.e. pre-1967 Canadian) system of honours.

In 1973, the Queen held an investiture at Government House, Ottawa. She is seen investing the distinguished Canadian civil servant Jules Léger with the Order of Canada, continuing her role of recognising Canadians under the country's new distinctive honours system. The next year Mr Léger was appointed by the Queen as her Governor-General for Canada, receiving precedence and the prefix Right Honourable from Her Majesty

In 1990 the Queen invested the new Governor-General, Ray Hnatyshyn with the Order of Canada at her home of Sandringham.

In 1987 the Queen signed the Royal Warrant augmenting Her Majesty's Provincial Arms in Right of British Columbia at a ceremony in Victoria.

7

"I Dedicate Myself Anew"

Silver Jubilee, 1977

Jubilees have their origins in Jewish tradition. The Old Testament relates that they were to be held every fiftieth year in thanksgiving to God. The Catholic Church established jubilees as holy years in 1300, originally at 100-year intervals, and later at 50 and 25 years. The year included indulgences for pilgrimages to Rome and other holy sites. Drawing on these precedents, royal jubilees began as 50-year observances (golden jubilees). The first celebration in the Commonwealth was the golden jubilee of King George III, who reigned for fifty-nine years and three months. His jubilee in 1809 marked the beginning of the fiftieth year of his reign, as in the Jewish tradition. The festivities included a private service at Windsor, a grand fête, a fireworks display and a procession to St Paul's in London for a service of thanksgiving,

The official British Silver Jubilee photograph of the Queen, taken at Buckingham Palace in the fall of 1976.

followed by a dinner. The celebrations were held over a few days and the continuity from those events to later jubilees is obvious.

Queen Victoria celebrated her golden jubilee at the conclusion of the fiftieth year of her reign and her diamond jubilee at the conclusion of her sixtieth year. These celebrations also took place over a few days but, unlike that of King George III, involved Empire representatives coming to London, including of course those from the Dominion of Canada which was now a self-governing part of the Empire.

King George V was the first monarch to celebrate a silver jubilee (25 years), held in 1935 at the suggestion of his consort, the indomitable Queen Mary. The celebration lasted about a month and marked the completion of twenty-five years. It was a great success, in a time of economic depression and international uncertainty, and the people's loyalty elicited in the modest but grand old king a heart-felt response: "I am beginning to think they must really like me for myself". It was readily agreed that a Silver Jubilee celebration also would be held for Queen Elizabeth II in 1977.

There was one great change from 1887, 1897 or 1935 however. While representative groups from the Sovereign's realms in those years attended the jubilee celebrations in London, for the people at home in the realms outside Britain there could only be vicarious celebrations. By 1977 the constitutional independence of these realms and modern transportation made it possible, necessary and desired by both the Queen and her peoples that she should celebrate her Jubilee personally in each realm, in addition to being joined in London by the representatives of those lands.

The Silver Jubilee badge, used throughout the Commonwealth—at events, on programmes, on products and on commemoratives—to celebrate the historic year.

This development also meant that the celebrations would not last a few days or even a month but for nearly a year. They would begin at the conclusion of twenty-five years of Her Majesty's reign on 6 February 1977 and continue throughout the twenty-sixth year until the fall. The issue of whether jubilees are celebrated during the twenty-fifth, fiftieth or sixtieth year respectively, in the Jewish tradition, or after the completion of the required number of years, and the changing policy in our own history, does cause some confusion. In the Canadian National Exhibition grounds in Toronto stands a giant flagpole, erected, as a Silver Jubilee commemoration, in the summer of 1977. The officials responsible obviously thought that the Jubilee year must be the twenty-fifth year of the reign. The plaque erroneously claims it was erected in the twenty-fifth year of Her Majesty's reign (rather than the twenty-sixth in which it actually was).

The Jubilee Year of 1977 may perhaps be conveniently divided into five parts, which reflected Her Majesty's status and role in the Commonwealth. Around 6 February, the date of her accession, were a number of subdued, essentially private and/or religious observances to mark the beginning of the Jubilee and also, of course, the twenty-fifth anniversary of King George VI's death. This was followed in the spring by a tour of Australia, New Zealand and the Pacific realms of the Commonwealth. The summer encompassed two parts— the major celebrations in London, which played its role as not only the capital of the United Kingdom but as the capital of the Commonwealth, and a series of seven tours to Scotland, Northern Ireland, Wales and the regions of England. Finally in the fall there was the tour to Canada and the Caribbean to complete the celebrations.

In her 1976 Christmas message the Queen set the tone for the Jubilee celebrations that were to follow. "Next year", she said "is a rather special one for me and I would like my Silver Jubilee year also to become a special one for people who find themselves the victims of human conflict. The gift I would most value next year is that reconciliation should be found wherever it is needed. A reconciliation which would bring peace and security to families and neighbours at present suffering and torn apart." As the year unfolded, both Her Majesty and many of her subjects tried to make that wish come true.

On the morning of 6 February the Royal Family attended a special memorial service for King George VI at St George's Chapel, Windsor Castle, where the late king was interred. It was a most appropriate beginning to the Jubilee as it recalled the fact that the Jubilee also marked the death of the King—"The King is Dead! Long Live the Queen!" was the ceremonial exclamation of 6 February 1952.

The evening of 6 February there was a changed emphasis to celebration from remembrance with a Jubilee concert at the Royal Albert Hall, which the Royal Family attended and at which there was the first performance of the Jubilee Hymn. The next day there was the start of a two-day Silver Jubilee Cavalcade of 400 pre-World War II Rolls-Royces, plus additional post-war vehicles, in Windsor Home Park. The Queen reviewed the parade of cars on the first day of the event, which drew over 50,000 spectators. Then Her Majesty and His Royal Highness were off to the Pacific.

The Queen inspects a 1905 Silver Ghost Rolls-Royce at Windsor Castle. The parade of Rolls-Royces was one of the first Jubilee events.

The Queen and Duke of Edinburgh's tour of the Pacific was a long one, almost two months in duration—twice as long as the entire celebration of the Silver Jubilee of the Queen's grandfather, King George V. It lasted from 9 February until 31 March and included Western Samoa, Tonga, Fiji, New Zealand, Australia and Papua-New Guinea.

First on the agenda was Western Samoa, and it was Her Majesty's first visit to the Commonwealth monarchy (with a head of state separate from the Queen). Tonga, also a separate monarchy in the Commonwealth, was next on the itinerary. The Queen was welcomed by King Taufa'ahau Tupou IV, who went on a crash diet before the visit to reduce his weight from 462 lb. to 392 lb., but abandoned the diet for the banquet in honour of Her Majesty, which consisted of lobster, prawns, baby pigs, turkey and tropical fruits. King Tupou's mother, the revered Queen Salote, had attended the Queen's Coronation in 1953 where she was a great favourite with the crowds. In Fiji, the next stop and a realm of the Queen's, Her Majesty sipped from the ceremonial cup of Kava, which is a root-drink noted for numbing the mouth.

New Zealand saw the Queen for the fifth time and the Duke for the sixth time when they arrived for their Jubilee tour, landing in Auckland on 22 February for a two-week stay until 7 March. The emphasis in the first week, which was spent in the North Island was informality. The activities laid out for Her Majesty included several walkabouts, allowing her to meet as many people as possible, horse races at Te Rapa, drives through rich farmlands, and a ceremony at Gisborne where a thousand Maoris greeted the Queen they know as the "Rare White Heron".

At Wellington the ceremonial side continued when the Queen first unveiled the new parliament building and then opened the New Zealand Parliament. The royal couple then travelled to the less populous South Island for the last six days of their tour, where they visited Christchurch, Blenheim, Timaru, Dunedin and Invercargill.

Australia had been awash in political controversy since 1975 when the Governor-General dismissed the Labour government led by Gough Whitlam, and Whitlam, a republican in any case, used the incident to attack the monarchy. On the eve of the Queen's arrival he made fun of the fact that the Solomon Islands which was gaining its independence in 1978, had opted to become a monarchy. Still smarting over his rejection by the people of Australia and showing a lack of respect for the decision of the people of the Solomon Islands, the now opposition leader referred to the fact that the Queen would be assuming the title of "Queen of the Solomon Islands", "What next?" he sneered, "Queen of Sheba?"

When the Queen arrived in Sydney, capital of New South Wales, and Australia's largest city, to begin her sixth trip to the country, nearly 30,000 people greeted the Royal Yacht in Sydney Harbour. While there were demonstrations against the Monarchy in the national capital of Canberra, in Brisbane (Queensland), and in Melbourne (Victoria), the general reception in all three cities was warm and enthusiastic. This was repeated in Hobart, the capital of Tasmania, in Adelaide (South Australia), in Darwin (Northern Territory), and Perth (West-

For the Queen's spring tour of Australia to mark her Jubilee, thousands of Australians filled the streets for her walkabouts.

ern Australia). Unlike the subsequent fall tour to Canada, the Queen thus visited the Commonwealth capital and each of the state capitals of Australia, though she did not open any parliaments. She did however use the occasion to invest the former prime minister, Sir Robert Menzies, as a Knight of the Order of Australia.

In between the visits to Darwin and Perth the *Britannia* took the Queen and Duke to Papua New Guinea. In 1975 the country had gained its independence from Australia and despite the desire of the Australian government led by Gough Whitlam that it opt for republicanism, it chose to become a monarchy under Queen Elizabeth II. Perhaps it was as much this

snub to his republican sensibilities as the clash with the Governor-General that led to Whitlam's sarcastic and racially patronising remarks about the Queen and the Solomon Islands

The Jubilee festivities continued back in the United Kingdom after Her Majesty's return. On 4 May she received an address of loyalty from the Lords and the House of Commons. In her reply, she alluded to the tension in the United Kingdom concerning devolution and separatism in both Northern Ireland and Scotland:

"I cannot forget that I was crowned Queen of the United Kingdom of Great Britain and Northern Ireland ... Perhaps this Jubilee is a time to remind ourselves of the benefits which

As this photograph from the Australian tour illustrates, the Jubilee was an event celebrated together by all generations of the Queen's subjects in all parts of the Commonwealth.

union has conferred at home and in our international dealings, on the inhabitants of all parts of the United Kingdom."

The remarks, while hardly provocative, coming from the Sovereign of the United Kingdom, who naturally wished the country to stay together, as on other occasions she has also expressed the desire for Canada to stay together, nevertheless upset Scottish Nationalists. Most people, however, thought Her Majesty's remarks were appropriate and took them to heart.

The seven tours of the United Kingdom began on 16 May and ended on 11 August.

Over the three months the Queen and Duke of Edinburgh travelled 8,000 miles and undertook eight hundred engagements. They visited thirty-six counties and it was estimated that the Queen shook 5,000 hands, changing her gloves four times a day.

The tours started with a greeting from 100,000 Glaswegians as the Queen rode in the Scottish State Coach to a thanksgiving service in Glasgow Cathedral. The Scottish tour also included Cumbernauld, Stirling, Dundee, Perth and Aberdeen. In the Scottish capital of Edinburgh the Queen installed the Prince of Wales as a Knight of the Order of the Thistle, the premier order of the Queen for Scotland and attended the opening of the General Assembly of the Church of Scotland. At the time, more than twenty years before the re-establishment of the Scottish Parliament, this annual event was the closest thing to the opening of parliaments which the Queen performed in London and in the capitals of her realms around the world.

After the major Jubilee celebrations in London in early June, the Queen and Duke continued the rounds of British tours. In late June it was to Wales and Northwest England There were three tours in July—one to Northumberland, Newcastle and Durham, a second to East Anglia and a third to the West Midlands. The sixth was a three-day tour of the West Country in early August and the last was in mid-August to Ulster. The security was

In Glasgow the Queen began her Jubilee tour of Scotland, the first of several throughout the United Kingdom in the summer of 1977. Happy Glaswegians greet their monarch.

intense for this Northern Ireland visit as the IRA had promised "a jubilee bomb blitz to be remembered". It never happened and the Queen was cordially received at the engagements she attended in Belfast and Coleraine. But Her Majesty was obliged to travel by helicopter for added safety and demonstrators and rioters made their presence felt in the troubled province on the days of the Queen's visit, though not in her immediate vicinity. Among those whom Her Majesty received were Mairead Corrigan and Betty Williams, the founders of the Ulster Peace Movement, who represented the hopes of those seeking a solution to the Irish problems that was not based on violence. Yet hours after the royal couple had departed the University of Ulster at Coleraine, where she walked among the people, a bomb exploded on the university grounds. While the Jubilee festivities spanned months in time and continents in space, 6 to 11 June in London and Windsor was the focus of the year's events. On the evening of the sixth in Windsor Great Park the Queen lit the first of a chain of 102 bonfires across Britain. They recalled the bonfires lit in the time of Elizabeth I to warn of the Spanish Armada and many were located in the same places. The chain of bonfires actually spread beyond Britain to as far away as Australia. Despite the evening rain thousands gathered in the fields for a glimpse of the Queen and other members of the Royal Family.

The Gold State Coach, not used since the Queen's Coronation in 1953, was brought out for the Silver Jubilee procession from Buckingham Palace to St Paul's Cathedral on 7 June.

The next day in London was the grand procession from Buckingham Palace to St Paul's Cathedral for the Jubilee Thanksgiving Service. It continued the tradition begun by King George III at his Jubilee and the cavalcade was surpassed only by that of the Coronation year. First came a fleet of six carriages, conveying members of the Royal Family accompanied by escorts of the Household Cavalry, then the carriage of the Queen Mother, Prince Andrew and Prince Edward, and one for Her Majesty's staff, also escorted by the Household Cavalry.

The Queen's Carriage Procession was led by mounted contingents from the Royal Canadian Mounted Police, the Royal Army Veterinary Corps, the Corps of Royal Military Police and

A contingent from the Royal Canadian Mounted Police escorted the Queen's carriage, and the open windows of London's buildings were filled with thousands of cheering subjects, adding their voices to those of the throngs on the streets.

coat and matching pleated dress. Canadians recognised it as the outfit she had first worn the year before in Montreal to open the Olympic Games. The Duke of Edinburgh was in naval uniform. Immediately behind the carriage rode the heir to the Throne, Prince Charles, Prince of Wales in his uniform as Colonel of the Welsh Guards. His horse was *Centenial*, which the R.C.M.P. had presented to the Queen in 1973.

Following the Gold State Coach were four more carriages with members of the Queen's Household, the fourth division of the Household Cavalry and two detachments of the King's Troop, Royal Horse Artillery.

The parade route was lined by the soldiers of the Queen, from five-foot Gurkhas to six-foot-plus Guardsmen. Thronged behind the troops, straining for a glimpse of the Queen, hands waving, cameras snapping, were hundreds of thousands of the peoples of the Queen,

two detachments of the King's Troop, Royal Horse Artillery in addition to two divisions of the Household Cavalry.

In the Gold State Coach, constructed for King George III and last used by the Queen at her Coronation, rode the Queen and the Duke of Edinburgh. The coach proceeded at a slow walking pace, the only speed it is capable of, and swayed as it moved (it was constructed before modern suspension was invented). Embellished in gold and ornate paintings it is one of the most magnificent transportation vehicles in the world and it glistened that day despite the grey skies.

The Queen was wearing a soft rose-pink silk

A wave from the Queen as the Gold State Coach passed was a silver moment for many spectators, who good-naturedly struggled with their neighbours to snap a photograph of the occasion through the crowds.

157

More huge crowds lined the route of the Queen as she walked to the Guildhall from St Paul's Cathedral. Everywhere there were crowds.

drawn together from diverse lands to share this day with their Sovereign.

After the service at St Paul's, the Queen and Duke walked through Cheapside to the Guildhall for the luncheon given for the Commonwealth by the Mayor and Corporation of the City of London. The heads of government of 32 countries in the Commonwealth were in attendance, and would meet again the next day for the Commonwealth Conference. In her speech at the Guildhall, the Queen touched on the heritage of the association, her role in it and recalled her speech of 1947.

... Guildhall, in the City of London, has seen many national and Commonwealth celebrations but in all its long history it has never witnessed the presence of so many Commonwealth Heads of Government. ...

During these last 25 years I have travelled widely throughout the Commonwealth as its Head. And during those years I have seen, from a unique position of advantage, the last great phase of the transformation of the Empire into the Commonwealth and the transformation of the Crown from an emblem of Dominion into a symbol of free and voluntary association. In all history this has no precedent....

At this moment of my Silver Jubilee I want to thank all those in Britain and the Commonwealth who through their loyalty and friendship have given me strength and encouragement during these last 25 years. ...

My Lord Mayor, when I was 21, I pledged my life to the service of our people, and I asked for God's help to make that vow. Although that vow was made 'in my salad day when I was green with judgement' I do not regret nor retract one word of it.

When the royal couple returned to the Palace the crowds had become even larger and thousands gathered at the railings of Buckingham Palace for the balcony appearance of the Royal Family. The BBC broadcast the day's proceedings around the world to an estimated audience of 500 million people.

The next day the Queen gave a reception for the Commonwealth Heads of Government at Buckingham Palace, where the band played Mozart, Beethoven, Strauss and Gilbert & Sullivan. On 9 June the River Thames took over as the focus of the celebrations. The Queen and Duke made a progress by river launch in the morning and afternoon, and in the evening, along with another huge crowd of their subjects, watched a river pageant and the greatest fireworks display ever seen in London. Two days later a special Silver Jubilee performance of the annual Trooping the Colour to mark the Queen's Official Birthday in the United Kingdom completed the major events of the week, though later in the month the Queen attended the traditional naval review at Spithead, where 180 warships had gathered.

Public celebrations often have an official and an unofficial face to them, with the latter sometimes overshadowing the former in the public imagination or the lingering folk memories. Such was the story of the Silver Jubilee. Economic times had not been good in mid-seventies Britain and some officials feared that Britons would resent rather than rejoice in the Jubilee. It proved a hollow fear.

The public were not merely content with the multitude of official ceremonies in which they however readily participated. Communities started organising street parties to celebrate the Jubilee, each distinctive, to reflect the character of their neighbourhood, but sharing the essential qualities of being held on the street and involving food, entertainment, and fellowship. The idea caught on and spread not only throughout Britain but also to the Commonwealth. Even traditionally staid Toronto in Canada sprouted street parties that summer. The Jubilee street parties remain for many the defining celebration of the Queen's Silver Jubilee.

Canadians began celebrating their Queen's Silver Jubilee early and in many ways. Religious observances began on 6 February itself, which was a Sunday, and continued through the remainder of the winter, the spring and the summer. Given the religious diversity of Canadians these services took place in churches of different denominations and in synagogues, some being denominational observances and others being ecumenical or inter-faith. The Governor-General and Lieutenant-Governors were often present at these events.

The most imaginative celebration was perhaps that in the province of Newfoundland.

Jacqueline Barlow of Newfoundland posed with the province's Declaration of Loyalty, one of the many imaginative projects undertaken to celebrate the Silver Jubilee in Canada.

Canada had been created as an act of loyalty by those British North Americans who did not sub-scribe to the 1776 Declaration of Independence of the rebels to the south, who subsequently became the citizens of the United States. The bicentenary of American independence was celebrated in 1976 and the Queen had paid a visit to her family's erstwhile subjects and Canada's neighbours to mark the occasion. As a good natured riposte to the previous year's festivities, Jacqueline Barlow of Newfoundland began a Silver Jubilee Declaration of Loyalty in the province. When it was eventually presented to the Queen it contained over 300,000 signatures—almost the entire population of Newfoundland!

On the other coast of Canada the British Columbia government marked the Jubilee by sending the historic *Royal Hudson* train on a special Jubilee trip down the west coast of the

Canadian first day cover celebrating the Queen's Silver Jubilee displays the special commemorative stamp issued that year in addition to the regular definitive stamps that featured the Queen.

A Silver Jubilee wall mural at the Toronto Board of Education, created by school children, displayed scenes of the Queen throughout the Commonwealth.

United States, complete with replicas of the Crown Jewels, to highlight the distinctive character of Pacific Canada from Pacific United States.

From St John's to Victoria and Toronto to Yellowknife, Silver Jubilee rose gardens, hymn and poetry contests, art and heritage exhibits, garden parties and street parties, commemorative coins (courtesy of the Royal Canadian Mint) and commemorative stamps (courtesy of Canada Post), and addresses of loyalty from the Senate and House of Commons down through provincial legislative assemblies and municipal councils to private organisations were but some of the many ways Canadians participated in the Jubilee festivities and paid tribute to their Queen.

Other Canadians, including of course the Royal Canadian Mounted Police, managed to travel to London for the June festivities. HMCS *Huron* represented Canada in the naval review at Spithead and an Upper Canada pageant was staged in England in August as part of the celebrations.

While Canadians had been celebrating the Queen's Jubilee in many ways and for many months by the time Her Majesty arrived in Canada in October, the trip was the highlight of the year for Canadians. Unfortunately it was limited to six days in Ottawa, although Ontario and other provinces had asked the Canadian government to arrange for a longer sojourn. But

During her Ottawa Silver Jubilee festivities the Queen attended a rowing regatta at Dow's Lake and went on a walkabout in the sunshine.

A smile from the Queen during another walkabout, this time in the rain, on Parliament Hill, following the outdoor Jubilee thanksgiving service.

series of personal encounters with Canadians. These included a greeting at Ottawa's city hall, a wreath-laying at the National War Memorial, a luncheon for athletes, a game of Canadian football at Lansdowne Park, a Silver Jubilee rowing regatta at Dow's Lake, a visit to the RCMP barracks where she renewed acquaintances with Mounties who had participated in her Coronation, and a multicultural performance at the civic centre. One characteristic of most of these events was the enthusiastic participation of young people who had not been alive at either the Coronation or the 1957 visit to Ottawa.

In the city which had initiated the royal walkabout in 1939, the spontaneous and genuine love between the Queen and her people was amply demonstrated at the Interfaith Jubilee Thanksgiving Service held on Parliament Hill the morning of Sunday, 16 October. Ottawa came alive as London had in June. In her walkabout after the service Her Majesty ignored the red carpet laid down the middle of the centre walkway on Parliament Hill to walk

thousands of Canadians gathered in Ottawa, many travelling from across the country to be there, as the Commonwealth had earlier gathered in London.

As had been the case twenty years before on her first trip to the Dominion as Sovereign, the 1977 tour took place in the glory of a Canadian autumn. Her Majesty arrived in Ottawa on 14 October and began a

Procession of the Queen and Duke of Edinburgh through the Senate Chamber in Ottawa on 18 October.

closer to her people who had gathered on the hill, stopping to talk to as many as she could.

The thousands in the crowd included many bearing signs of greeting—one in French carried by a group of young people proclaimed that "Young Canada loves the Queen". Another read "God Save The Queen" in Portuguese. Ottawa was not blessed with Queen's weather that day however and the multitude had waited in a cold rain, before, during and after the service.

That evening Her Majesty addressed her people at a state dinner in her honour which was televised and broadcast across the country. In her speech, the Queen spoke about the combined efforts of Native, English, French and other Canadians in building Canada into one of the great countries of the world. She also expressed her own particular insight,

"My family's association with this country over many generations allows me to see and appreciate Canada from another viewpoint, that of history."

The Queen's remarks were the more forceful as she delivered them flawlessly in both the official languages of the country and also reflected her general wish for the Jubilee, "That reconciliation should be found wherever it is needed". The Prime Minister, Rt Hon. Pierre Trudeau, continued this theme by announcing that in honour of the Queen's Jubilee a trust fund was being established to enable selected

The Queen and the Duke stand before the Thrones of Canada against an austere backdrop of white stone, producing a scene of true regal splendour—simple yet majestic.

young Canadians to understand better each other's language and culture.

The opening of the Canadian Parliament in 1977 on the eighteenth, as in 1957, was a scene of brilliant mediaeval pageantry with a serious contemporary significance. Elizabeth II of Canada read from her throne the speech opening the Third Session of the Thirtieth Parliament before her subjects in the Senate Chamber and across Canada via television and radio. Her Majesty was attired in a long, white silk dress with gold French lace that, while contemporary, also made an allusion to a stylised aboriginal dress of doeskin and beads. Elizabeth II looked unmistakably like a Canadian Queen. The appearance was completed by a diamond tiara that had belonged to Queen Mary and the Sovereign's insignia of the Order of the Garter, the Order of Canada and the Order of Military Merit of Canada.

The Queen was accompanied in the pageant by her consort, Prince Philip, Duke of Edinburgh,

The Queen opened the Canadian Parliament in 1977, as she had in 1957, and declared: "I dedicate myself anew to the people and the nation I am proud to serve".

stone, producing a scene of true regal splendour—simple yet majestic. The Senate Chamber, though built in the twentieth century, was mediaeval gothic and the walls bore the historic paintings of Canada's effort in the First World War; the order of procession was fourteenth century; the dress of the Officers of State was late eighteenth and early nineteenth century, when parliamentary government took root in Canada; yet it was all part of the business of Parliament in 1977.

Outside on Parliament Hill ten thousand Canadians had gathered to watch Her Majesty's arrival and the inspection of a guard of honour from the Royal 22e Régiment du Canada. A fly-past by jets from the Canadian Forces Air Command was part of the arrival ceremony, but the Canadian land added its own touch. An unrehearsed and unexpected salute to the Queen was provided when, in a great, shifting "V" formation, a "squadron" of Canada geese preceded the official fly-past and made its contribution to the pageantry on the Hill.

Privy Counsellor of Canada, and Colonel-in-Chief of The Royal Canadian Regiment, dressed in the ceremonial uniform of Canada's senior infantry regiment.

There was a timelessness about the scene that of course had not altered in twenty years and which reflected the partnership of the ages which the Monarchy incarnates and which the Jubilee was celebrating. The royal couple were seated on the red-cushioned, wooden thrones of Canada against an austere backdrop of white

The Queen's speech touched upon Her Majesty's personal relationship with Canadians, which she was emphasising in this stay. She noted that in her tours she had met thousands of her subjects from all parts of Canada, in all walks of life, and of all ages. She reiterated her concern for young people.

The new official photograph of the Queen and Duke of Edinburgh, taken at Rideau Hall the day the Queen opened Parliament, completed the Canadian celebration of the Queen's Silver Jubilee.

"A generation of Canadians has been born and grown to maturity during my reign. I know you will understand when I say that I have a special interest in these young men and women, contemporaries of our own children. They are people made strong by the achievements of their parents and grandparents, but not imprisoned by the prejudices of the past."

The Queen ended her speech by setting out her own course for the years ahead and returned to a theme that had characterised her life from before her crowning.

"It is apparent to thoughtful Canadians everywhere that this is a time of great decisions for Canada, a time for rediscovering the strength and potential of a marvellously free and caring society. That rediscovery will require that Canadians rededicate themselves to each other's well being, just as I dedicate myself anew to the people and the nation I am proud to serve."

The last day in Ottawa, Wednesday 19 October, before her departure for the Caribbean, the Queen walked through the grounds of Rideau Hall, covered with a carpet of fallen autumn leaves, and planted a tree to commemorate her stay, not far from where her father had planted a tree in 1939. And then she departed from Canada.

The royal couple arrived by aeroplane in Nassau, where they joined the Royal Yacht *Britannia*. The festivities in the Bahamas were characterised by a junkaroo, a traditional calypso celebration featuring exotic costumes and dancing. Some dancers were dressed as beefeaters and others as giant crowns, lions and unicorns. The next day the Queen opened the Bahamian Parliament, as she continued the constitutional pattern around the Commonwealth. From Nassau the Queen and Duke sailed to the British Virgin Islands where Her Majesty opened the smallest parliament among her lands—a ten person legislative assembly, then went on to Antiqua, Mustique (where they stayed with Princess Margaret at her home for two days), and concluded the West Indies tour in Barbados on 1 November.

The day after the Queen returned to the United Kingdom she opened the British Parliament in a ceremony that effectively ended the year's Silver Jubilee celebrations. Her Majesty began her speech: "My Lords and members of the House of Commons, my husband and I look back with delight and gratitude on the events which marked my Silver Jubilee at home and overseas and the visits we made to many parts of the United Kingdom and the Commonwealth."

Although the Silver Jubilee commemorated the anniversary of the Queen's Accession, the event echoed the Coronation—the pageantry and processions in London and Commonwealth capitals, the fireworks and bonfires, the naval review, the ceremonies in churches and parliamentary chambers, the appearance of the Gold State Coach, and the crowds—everywhere the crowds.

In that way the Jubilee linked two generations. It recalled for the first, those who had lived through that great event in the life of the Commonwealth which the Coronation was, the excitement and meaning of that day. For the second generation, who were born after the Coronation or were too young to remember it, it provided a taste, almost as good, of that earlier occasion and gave them their own celebration of a lifetime to enjoy and savour in future years. The Jubilee also linked the generations in its own right and in that way differed from ordinary celebrity events. Most celebrities appeal to one element of society, be it one age group or people of a particular interest. One important significance of the Jubilee, reflecting the larger significance of the Crown itself, was that it involved people of all ages, interests and nationalities, within the Commonwealth and beyond, in a common enterprise. The faces of both the participants and the spectators reflected that diversity and remain one of the lingering memories of that fascinating year.

THE QUEEN'S FAMILY AND CANADA

Members of the Queen's family play an important role assisting Her Majesty, by carrying out duties in Canada on behalf of the Queen, and strengthening the place of the Royal Family in Canadian life through their own particular interests.

The Duke of Edinburgh also travels to Canada on his own. In 1992, in Alberta, he presented Duke of Edinburgh Award certificates to young Canadians. The international scheme was created by the Duke to encourage involvement by young people in their communities.

The Duke of Edinburgh has always been a great support to Her Majesty, accompanying her on most of her tours of Canada.

The Prince of Wales receives flowers from four-year-old Maya Bhanghoo in March 1998 while visiting St Vincent's Hospital, Langara, Vancouver.

In 1991 the Princess Royal chatted with representatives of the Black Cultural Centre for Nova Scotia in Dartmouth, with a map of Black migration in the background.

The Duke of York attended school at Lakefield, near Peterborough in Canada in 1977. In 1985 he returned to Peterborough to unveil an historic site plaque at the Koh-i Noor hydraulic lift lock.

In August 2001, an informally dressed Earl of Wessex, the Queen's youngest son, visited historic Fort Edmonton.

The Queen Mother returned to Canada many times after her 1939 tour as Queen. In 1979 she arrived at Queen's Park in Toronto for an outdoor reception on the grounds of the Provincial Parliament.

The Queen's sister, Princess Margaret, talks with Sharon Solomon, originator of the Magic Castle play house for children of cancer patients at the Princess Margaret Hospital in Toronto in 1996.

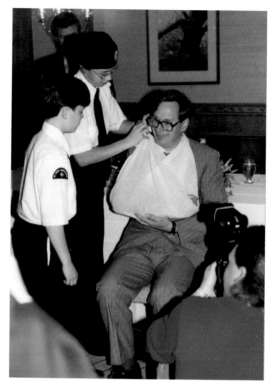

The Duke of Gloucester, first cousin of the Queen, serves as an "accident victim" while members of the St John Ambulance Brigade demonstrate first aid skills during a Toronto visit in 1990. The Duke is Grand Prior of the Order of St John.

Countess Mountbatten of Burma, a cousin of the Queen, presents the 1993 Queen Elizabeth II Cup for show jumping at the Spruce Meadows competition in Calgary.

8

"I am getting to know our country rather well"

Elizabeth II, Edmonton, 1978

1978–1991

It was widely observed after the Silver Jubilee that the celebrations made the Queen appear a strong individual in her own right. Her Majesty even received a compliment to that effect from an old critic, Lord Altrincham, now transformed by egalitarianism —he had renounced his peerage—into plain John Grigg. "The Queen" Grigg wrote "is far more effective and confident than in the early years of her reign, and there is no longer any question … of her husband's having to carry the show". Had the second Annigoni portrait of the Sovereign, the picture so disliked when it appeared in 1970, been painted at this moment, its double message of the strength and isolation of Queenship might have struck a more positive chord.

The Queen exhibited this newly perceived strength in her Commonwealth role. Since 1965, Rhodesia had been a major problem for the family of nations. To perpetuate the supremacy of its small white minority—outnumbered 25 to 1 by Blacks—Ian Smith, the Rhodesian Premier, declared unilateral independence that year, rejecting negotiated legal independence with majority rule. Smith, hoping to keep the support of whites loyal to the Crown, pretended his quarrel was with the United Kingdom Government not the Queen. But Her Majesty called his bluff. In a personal letter to the Rhodesian leader, in which she told him how she had followed the discussions of the two governments "with the closest concern" and cherished memories of her own visit to Rhodesia,

Her Majesty unveils the plaque marking her opening of the Queen Elizabeth II Court at Regina's City Hall 1978.

she ended by saying "I should be glad if you would accept my own good wishes and convey them to all my peoples in your country, whose welfare and happiness I have closely at heart". "All my peoples" meant black as well as white. The Queen left Smith in no doubt he could claim loyalty to the Crown and defend white supremacy at the same time.

By 1979 the situation had dragged on for fourteen years. Rhodesia was economically and socially isolated from the world, (which refused to recognise the puppet regime Smith had installed in Salisbury), and torn by a bitter guerrilla war. That year the Queen planned to attend the Commonwealth Heads of Government meeting in the Zambian capital Lusaka after a tour of Tanzania, Botswana and Malawi with the Duke and Prince Andrew. The new United Kingdom Prime Minister, Margaret Thatcher, declared in a speech in Australia that she felt the Queen should not go because of the security risk. Buckingham Palace immediately announced that the Queen had every intention of being present. Her Majesty had never been to Zambia and felt its President, Kenneth Kaunda, needed her support. She had also never been to a Heads of Government meeting in a Commonwealth republic.

It was Ghana all over again. The media whipped up a campaign of fear around the risks involved. Veiled threats of violence were made by Smith's puppet, Bishop Muzorewa. But the Queen remained adamant. She went. Almost the entire population of Lusaka turned out to greet her when she landed in Zambia at the end of July. Her visits before the Conference to the adjoining countries had been a triumph. At the Conference the Queen played a very important behind the scenes role. She urged Margaret Thatcher to avoid a Commonwealth breakup over Rhodesia, succeeded in getting the Nigerians to tone down threats to leave the Commonwealth and put pressure on Australia and Zambia to help find a solution. In fact she saved the Conference. Kaunda said later: "At the Lusaka meeting in 1979 she played a very vital role. The Queen is an outstanding diplomat; that's how she gets things done". Sir Shridath Ramphal, Secretary-General of the Commonwealth, confirmed this view adding succinctly: "She was diplomatically brilliant". Following Lusaka, a conference was held at Lancaster House, London. Legal independence for Rhodesia was successfully negotiated and the new country of Zimbabwe created on 17 April 1980, "a turning-point in the post-colonial history of southern Africa" as the Queen's biographer Sarah Bradford correctly describes it.

After celebrating Elizabeth II's Jubilee in October 1977, the Canadian Government introduced a measure into Parliament on 20 June 1978 to remove her in effect from the internal constitution of Canada. Though it took the public by surprise, the ill-fated Bill C-60 was the culmination of behind the scenes removal of the Queen's symbolic presence and the transfer of the exercise of many of the functions she had been carrying out since her Accession to the Governor-General—a process on which the Canadian electorate had never been consulted. Now the closet republicans in the Cabinet and civil service felt confident enough to come out into the open. Bill C-60 proposed the virtual dismemberment of the institutions so carefully and deliberately chosen for Canada in 1867. For their Kingdom of Canada, the Fathers of Confederation, both English-speaking and French-speaking, wanted the Sovereign to do as much as could be done in a shared monarchy at a time of limited communications.

Bill C-60 would have abolished the Royal Prerogative, removed the Queen as one of the three parts of the Parliament of Canada, stripped her of the Command-in-Chief

which is vested in her and ended her power to appoint her personal representative, the Governor-General. In short it left Her Majesty with no functions whatever as Queen of Canada. The

At Vegreville, Alberta, in 1978, the Queen saw the world's largest Easter Egg, a creation of the extensive local Ukrainian community for the centenary of the Royal Canadian Mounted Police five years before.

Governor-General was to have precedence—over the Queen?—"as the First Canadian" but—

173

most insulting of all—the Queen was to be allowed to exercise the "powers, authorities or functions *of the Governor-General* under this Act", when and if present in the country. Clearly the object of the proposed legislation was the creation of as much of a republican form of government as its drafters felt they could get away with. The bill included other strange proposals too. Only a person born in Canada would be able to become Governor-General. Two classes of Canadians were to exist: those born in the country and eligible for the Governor-Generalship, those ineligible by their birth outside Canada. Had the Bill become law, the present Governor-General of Canada, Adrienne Clarkson, could never have become Governor-General because she was born in a different part of the Commonwealth.

Quiet removal of symbols and surreptitious changes of practice, however, were not the same as a major onslaught on the Crown. Opposition quickly built up. Canada's best-known and most respected constitutional authority, Senator Eugene Forsey, called the measure "a mystic, moorish maze" and proceeded to dissect and discredit it, assisted by his own legal experts Professor David Kwavnic and Graham Eglington. A patriotic group, The Monarchist League of Canada, played an active and successful role in raising public consciousness about the threat to the Crown. Soon on the defensive, the Government claimed it was just writing down "current

practice", failing to mention that the Cabinet itself had created all the current practice that diminished the Queen's role which it now wanted to "write down". At the parliamentary hearings in the late summer and autumn of 1978, the respected former Governor-General, Roland Michener, appeared and said that the Queen's powers should only be reduced if Canadians wanted a republic.

The ten provincial premiers met in August 1978 in Regina and unanimously rejected the federal government's proposed reduction of the Queen's role in Canada. Even the separatist government of Quebec would not agree to the diminution. The Crown was shared by the federal level and the provinces, a Governor-General with powers in his own right would be a creature

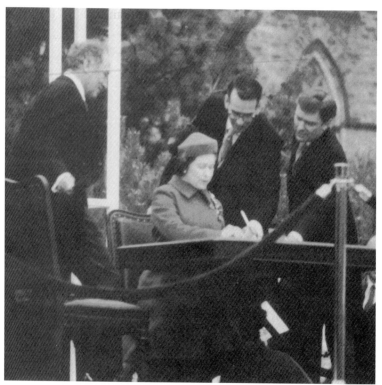

Proclaiming the revised Constitution of Canada, Parliament Hill, 17 April 1982.

of Ottawa. The Premier's communiqué of 10 August was a rationale of the Monarchy in a modern federal society that the Fathers of Confederation would have been proud of.

"Provinces agree," it said, "that the system of democratic parliamentary government requires an ultimate authority to ensure its responsible nature and to safeguard against abuses of power. That ultimate power must not be an instrument of the federal Cabinet. The Premiers, therefore, oppose constitutional changes that substitute for the Queen as ultimate authority, a Governor-General whose appointment and dismissal would be solely at the pleasure of the federal Cabinet."

While this passionate debate raged, the Queen herself was touring Saskatchewan and opening the XI Commonwealth Games in Edmonton. After landing in Newfoundland on 26 July, Her Majesty, accompanied by the Duke and her youngest son, Prince Edward making his tour debut, attended a federal-provincial dinner in St John's at which the Queen thanked the people of the province. "I was deeply moved" she told her audience "by the Declaration of Loyalty signed by three hundred thousand Newfoundlanders in my Silver Jubilee Year". Her Majesty reached the Saskatchewan capital 28 July for Regina's seventy-fifth anniversary and a visit to smaller communities south west of the city as well as Moose Jaw, marking its diamond jubilee, Saskatoon and Lloydminster.

"I am getting to know our country rather well" said the Queen at the Edmonton provincial dinner on 2 August, recalling how in just

Billboard decoration in Ottawa at the time of the Proclamation of the Constitution.

the last nine years she had officially visited all ten provinces. Next day she opened the Commonwealth Games, the first time in their history she had done so in person. "As Queen of Canada, I warmly welcome you and I know that all Canadians join me in wishing you good fortune" she told the athletes and spectators. Echoes of the debate on the Crown appeared in a third tour speech. Replying to the Prime Minister, Pierre Trudeau at a Government of Canada dinner 5 August the day before ending the tour, Her Majesty sounded a note of caution. "The spirit of renewal of the federation, evident throughout the land," she said "is proof that the desire for co-operation and understanding is as alive in Canada today as it ever was. But renewal implies a movement beyond the frontiers of current and past experience, and can therefore be fraught with difficulty".

Opposition to Bill C-60 reached such proportions that, at the First Ministers Conference in Toronto in February 1979, Pierre Trudeau

The Proclamation signed by Her Majesty.

announced the provisions affecting the Monarchy would be dropped. Intended or not, it was certainly ironic that the Prime Minister's statement came on 6 February, the anniversary of Elizabeth II's accession to the Throne. Unrest over this constitutional tinkering contributed to the Prime Minister's losses at the General Election that year which produced the brief minority government of Joe Clark. When Trudeau returned to power in the spring of 1980, he went off on a new tack—patriation of the Constitution, which was no threat to the Crown. So the Queen did find herself authorising a revised Canadian Constitution on Parliament Hill on a rainy 17 April 1982. It was not the constitution of Bill C-60 she proclaimed but another in which the Monarchy was entrenched and could only be altered with

the unanimous consent of Ottawa and all the provinces. The strength of Canada's fundamental institutions had withstood the assault.

Wiser from the experience of Bill C-60, Trudeau understood now how strongly many Canadians felt about the Crown. As Prime Minister he had developed a warm relationship with Elizabeth II and would publicly acknowledge how much she helped him with patriation. The Queen in turn made him a Companion of Honour in 1984, the year before he was admitted to the Order of Canada.

Even media hostile to the Crown admitted that the Queen saved the day for the government that April. Without her presence to symbolise the whole national community and provide a little class, the ceremony would have

Welcoming the Pope to the Palace. John Paul II was the first Pope ever to visit the United Kingdom. On leaving he invoked God's blessing on Prince Andrew serving in the Falklands campaign.

Prince Andrew, who was serving as a helicopter pilot in 829 Naval Air Squadron and flying Sea Kings from HMS *Invincible* in the United Kingdom expedition to regain the Falkland Islands recently invaded by Argentina. Back in London, the Queen welcomed Pope John Paul II—whom she had visited in 1980 two years after he became Pope—on his historic visit to the United Kingdom on 28 May. His Holiness in taking leave of her said "God bless your son" for Andrew was still on active service.

The post Jubilee years witnessed many changes in the Queen's family. On 27 August 1979 an IRA bomb killed Earl Mountbatten of Burma in Ireland. He had been a constant, if sometimes over zealous, counsellor for many years and an important link with the world outside the Palace. The Queen herself had six blanks fired at her on 13 June 1981 by a 17-year-old out on a "sad little mission of self-advertisement" as she was riding down the Mall at the Trooping the Colour. Doubly vulnerable at such a moment from riding side saddle, Her Majesty merely ducked, gave her black mare, the Canadian horse Burmese, a pat and rode on. Everyone was impressed by her self-possession and in Ottawa the House of Commons paused to pass a motion expressing its "admiration to Her Majesty for her outstanding courage during the ordeal".

been a fizzle, a non event. That weekend she was even able to express her sadness to René Lévesque, the Quebec separatist Premier, that his province had not given its consent to the patriation settlement.

It was not the happiest time for Her Majesty whose thoughts were constantly on her son,

*On the balcony of
Buckingham Palace
following the wedding
of the Prince of Wales
and Lady Diana
Spencer.*

Not quite a year later, on 9 July 1982, the Queen woke suddenly at 7:15 a.m. at the Palace on hearing her door opened and footsteps coming near her bed. Suddenly a man appeared and sat down on the bedside. He was barefoot, in jeans and t-shirt, a 35-year-old schizophrenic named Michael Fagan, who had got into the Palace once before, and this time came with the intention of telling the Queen his woes and then slashing his wrists in her presence. The Queen pressed her alarm bell and made two calls to the police but no one came. Fagan meanwhile talked away about his family problems without exhibiting any nervousness or worry. Finally he asked the Queen for a cigarette. This was a chance for her to get him into the corridor where she found a maid busy vacuuming. The maid took him into the pantry. A footman then appeared, having returned from walking

the dogs, followed by a policeman, but neither succeeded in removing Fagan. Finally when a plain clothes officer arrived, the Queen shouted "Get in there!" pointing to her room.

These incidents reflected the increasing violence of the world. The '80's, the decade of breakdancing, fax machines and compact discs, was a time of increasing social instability. People scarred from growing up in broken homes or in other ways were finding they were unable to cope with life and giving themselves up to despair, drugs and violence. The Queen experienced this social fallout at first hand when her two eldest sons chose brides from broken families. Pressure had been growing on the Prince of Wales to marry. There was a general feeling of satisfaction when his engagement to the lovely and apparently very shy Lady Diana Spencer, whom he had been seeing since 1980, was announced on 24 February 1981.

Lady Diana seemed a fiancée suitable in every respect. She was beautiful, her father Earl Spencer belonged to the old nobility and had served the Queen, many of her ancestors were royal.

Not long after a veteran Canadian journalist wrote pompously that of course no one today talks about the Monarchy at dinner, the Queen was declaring her consent to her son's marriage to her Canadian Privy Council. More than any royal event ever, the wedding of the Queen's eldest son Charles, Prince of Wales and Heir to the Throne, and Lady Diana Spencer at St Paul's Cathedral the following 29 July riveted the attention of the globe. Three quarters of a billion people watched it by satellite. Among those guarding the route outside the Cathedral for the wedding were soldiers of Toronto's Royal Regiment of Canada. Interest and excitement rose to a pitch. Young girls began Diana scrapbooks just at their grandparents had done Princess Elizabeth ones. And the royal wedding was indeed the main topic at dinner in countless households around the world.

Though the '80's began with the Queen in the ascendant, they were to be the decade of Diana. The wedding made the new Princess of Wales a world figure and when on 21 June 1982 she gave birth to Prince William her star rose even higher. The popularity of the Monarchy equaled that at the time of the Coronation and Jubilee. It took the Queen a while to realise how scarred the newest member of the family was by the sad breakup

of her parents' marriage when she was six. Diana suffered from moods of depression, she was stubborn, domineering, manipulative and jealous, as well as a fantasizer. She also had a psychological disorder called bulimia. On the other hand she had many appealing qualities including "an instinctive capacity to sense suffering and pain and a vocation to reach out towards the victim". These qualities and her appearance captured the heart of the public. The Queen expected to make a friend of her daughter-in-law, thinking they had country interests in common, whereas in fact Diana was thoroughly urbanised in interests and outlook. Charles and Diana's marriage was relatively stable for the first two years but its breakdown accelerated after the birth of their second son Prince Henry in 1984. Charles had never got over his early love for Camilla Shand, whom he met the year after he left Cambridge, and

The Queen presents Sir Shridath (Sonny) Ramphal, Secretary-General of the Commonwealth, with the insignia of the Order of Australia, 1982.

resumed relations with her when he felt his marriage was ended. None of this was known to the public and down to the end of the '80's the Prince and Princess appeared happily married. The Queen deplored what was happening but there was little she could do to prevent it. Her approach, stemming from temperament and policy, is always not to interfere in other people's lives, especially those of near and dear ones.

The Queen made Prince Andrew Duke of York on the eve of his wedding in July 1986. He had also found a bride from a divorced family. He met Miss Sarah Ferguson in 1985. The Duchess of York's background was the glamorous world of polo. She was thirteen when her mother left home. The Queen, who is

generally credited with a special affection for her second son, liked his bride and the Duchess of York got off to a good start. Her Majesty welcomed two new grandchildren with the birth of Princesses Beatrice and Eugenie of York in 1988 and 1990 respectively. Part of the problem of the Queen's two oldest sons was that both Charles and Andrew were children of a family where there hadn't been divorce and did not know how to deal with its effect on their spouses. They had other problems but they did not have that handicap.

At first the Queen went along with the increased media interest sparked by the advent of Diana, hoping it meant a return to the happy rapport between Palace and press of her father's

Despite wind and rain, crowds mass at the British Columbia Legislature in Victoria to welcome the Queen home to Canada in March 1983 following her widely covered visit to California.

Viewing the model of Canada Place which was to be built for Expo 86. Senator Jack Austen explains its features to the Queen and Duke of Edinburgh.

John Diefenbaker, had died 16 August. "Canada" said Her Majesty "has lost a man of great stature" who "was unswerving in his loyalty to the country and to the Crown". The same year a leading Canadian painter, Jean-Paul Lemieux, completed a picture of the Queen and Duke with the Parliament Buildings in the background, not a formal portrait but "affectionate memory images based on many impressions gathered over the years". The painting was purchased for Rideau Hall and is now at the Citadel in Quebec.

At the invitation of Ronald Reagan, the American President,

reign. When its pressures grew too great and were clearly upsetting the Princess of Wales, she tried to protect her daughter-in-law, even reprimanding the media hounds herself when they intruded at Sandringham. "Go away! Can't you leave us alone?" she shouted in a most uncharacteristic outburst. As a result of these experiences the Queen began to fight back against media intrusion. In 1987 she initiated a suit against the London tabloid the *Sun* for breach of copyright for publishing a letter by the Duke. She went to court again when the *Sun* published a purloined picture of her with Princess Beatrice, the Duke of York's elder daughter. The Queen won this case and the *Sun* had to pay two hundred thousand dollars to charity.

In 1979 the Queen marked the passing of an old friend from her early reign with a letter of condolence to the Governor-General. Her Prime Minister of the late '50's and early '60's,

Mother Teresa of Calcutta, one of the 20th century's great heroes, receiving the Order of Merit from Her Majesty the Queen on her 1985 visit to India.

the Queen visited his home state of California in February 1983, arriving on *Britannia* on the twenty-ninth. Canadians watched highlights of the visit each day on the television news. The worst winter storm in years with high winds and heavy rains lashed the California coast and riot-geared police held back demonstrators against United Kingdom policy in the Falklands and Northern Ireland. For a gala evening in Los Angeles arranged by Nancy Reagan, Her Majesty appeared in a chiffon dress strewn with embroidered California poppies. She and the Duke enjoyed a Mexican-style luncheon at Reagan's mountain top ranch which they only just reached after a hazardous drive over washed-out roads. Successful as it undoubtedly was, the tour was a strain and relief could be detected in the Queen's remark to journalists the last day of the visit: "I'm going home to Canada tomorrow".

As if to say "Good for you!" for their Queen's behaviour and make amends for all the trials and gaucheries she had just had to put up with—President Reagan at one point let her stand in the rain while he chatted to reporters—people turned out in droves when the Queen reached Victoria on 8 March for her three day stay in British Columbia. In Vancouver where she went next the crowds were six deep on 16th Avenue. The sun broke out and she was cheered wherever she appeared. It was hectic, happy and unforgettable. With charcteristic humility, she was surprised and touched by this unparalleled reception and the thousands of floral tributes she received. They had turned *Britannia* "into a floating flower shop" she said, alluding to the bouquets in her speech at the Government

of Canada dinner hosted by the perennial Pierre Trudeau, still Prime Minister. Her Majesty visited five cities—Nanaimo, Vernon, Kamloops, Kelowna and New Westminster—in one day. She opened Canada's first covered domed stadium in Vancouver before a crowd of 30,000 spectators and massed choir of 7,000 children. On this trip Her Majesty invited the people of the world to visit Vancouver for the 1986 World Fair.

The Queen of Canada walks with the President of France, François Mitterand, to a wreath laying at the Canadian War Cemetery, Beny-sur-Mer, France, at the 40th anniversary of D-Day.

Veterans of World War II regarded 1984 as a special year. It was the fortieth anniversary of D-Day, the beginning of the Allied liberation of

For the Loyalist bicentenary in New Brunswick, the Queen signed a Royal Warrant at Frederiction to make additions to her coat-of-arms for the province.

to cover Canadian landings on the beaches of Sicily.) The Queen did not disappoint her fellow veterans. She took part in the joint events at Utah Beach with six other sovereigns and presidents. Then she visited the Canadian War Cemetery at Beny-sur-Mer. As this is Canadian territory, she received the French President, François Mitterand, in her capacity as Queen of Canada. Her arrival in a small procession of cars was contrasted with the entourage of Mr Mitterand which not only extended to the horizon but also included an ambulance. The Queen escorted the French President through the cemetery to the cenotaph where they laid wreaths for Canada and France. Then she did a walkabout accompanied by Mr Trudeau, receiving a warm reception from her former companions in arms and their families.

The same year found the Queen in New Brunswick, Ontario and Manitoba. It was the bicentenary of the arrival of the Loyalists. The Loyalists were those stalwart Americans who took the side of the King during the American

western Europe. Commonwealth veterans expected their Queen and her husband to be in France with them to mark the anniversary. After all, was not the Queen herself a veteran of the Auxiliary Transport Service? And the Duke of active service in the Royal Navy? (It was the war that first brought Philip, as a Midshipman of 19, to Canada on HMS *Valiant* to transport Canadian troops to fight Hitler in 1941, and two years later saw him, as second in command on HMS *Wallace*, helping

The Queen wears the royal colours of Canada, white and red, for this picture with the new Canadian Cabinet at Rideau Hall, 1984.

Cutting the ribbon to inaugurate Ontario's "Loyalist Parkway" at Amherstview 1984.

Turner, in the recent election. The Queen's tour, originally scheduled for July, was postponed for the election, a decision that cost the ruling Liberals at least one seat. Mr Mulroney told the media before his private audience with the Queen that he was looking forward to a "discussion of substance" with her about "the general objectives the government plans to pursue". Next day Her Majesty and the Duke of Edinburgh flew to Fredericton where the Sovereign marked New Brunswick's 200th anniversary by signing a Royal Warrant adding a crest with the crown and supporters, compartment, motto and other devices to her arms for the province to highlight its establishment by Loyalists, Acadians and Native People.

At Ottawa on 26 September the Queen drove in the state landau from Rideau Hall to Parliament Hill for the official welcome. The Prime Minister in his speech noted that the Monarchy as "an institution has emerged stronger and more adaptable—and indeed more relevant to the needs of a united Canada".

Revolution, and were expelled from their homes by the victorious republicans, but came north to Canada to found two provinces, Ontario and New Brunswick. It was especially apt for the Queen to celebrate this event with their present day descendants. She arrived at Moncton, New Brunswick, on 24 September. Her first event was the unveiling of a plaque marking the centenary of St Joseph's Roman Catholic Church at Shediac. Later she gave a small dinner for, among others, her new Prime Minister, Brian Mulroney. The Progressive Conservatives lead by Mulroney had defeated the Liberal Prime Minister, John

The Queen officially opened the Peace Garden in Nathan Phillips Square 1984. The garden was meant to be "a lasting expression of Toronto's commitment to world peace".

Royal walkabout in "Little Italy", Toronto, 1984. The success of this event on the Queen's bicentennial tour of Ontario showed ethnic Canada's rapport with the Sovereign.

Canadian cultural festival and followed Her Majesty when she did a walkabout. She and the Duke also attended an Interfaith Thanksgiving Service at Maple Leaf Gardens along with 16,000 others.

On Monday 1 October she flew to visit Windsor. As the royal plane neared the city, Ronald Reagan, the American President, was flying to Detroit. The Queen took the opportunity to send him a message. "I was delighted to hear" it read "that metaphorically speaking we were only divided by a strip of water between our two countries. I send you our warm good wishes from Windsor. Elizabeth R." At Brantford she planted a white pine on the Six Nations Territory. Back in Toronto in the evening she was accompanied by the Prime Minister to the Government of Canada gala concert for 2,700 at Thomson Hall. There were more engagements on Tuesday and Wednesday was a rest day on *Britannia*.

Thursday Her Majesty flew to Sudbury to open Science North. She went on to Manitoba alone 4 October, the Duke having to return to London. Next day at Dauphin she attended the annual National Ukrainian Festival and at Brandon unveiled the cornerstone of the Queen Elizabeth II Music Building. At St Boniface on Saturday she saw an historic re-enactment to mark the coming of Pierre de La Vérendrye to the site of Fort Maurepas in 1734. The last big event of the tour was the Government of Canada dinner at the Winnipeg Convention Centre. In proposing the Loyal Toast the Prime

On the twenty-seventh the Queen visited the Loyalist cities of Cornwall, Prescott and Amherstview. At Cornwall she received a copy of the new history of the community and chatted with its author, the military historian Elinor Kyte Senior. She saw re-enacted at Amherstview the landing of the Loyalists and officially designated part of highway 33 the 'Loyalist Parkway'. After a day's rest the Queen sailed into Toronto harbour on *Britannia* 29 September.

The Toronto stay was a full one. The Queen attended a military tattoo before 50,000; dedicated a new air force memorial—quickly named 'Gumby goes to Heaven' from its advanced style of design; unveiled the City of Toronto's Peace Garden before a huge crowd at Nathan Phillips Square; and dedicated the Queen Elizabeth II Terrace Galleries at the Royal Ontario Museum. A special event was her visit to "Little Italy", as the Italian community on St Clair Avenue West in the city is known. Some 20,000 turned out to see "La Regina" at this Italian-

Minister told the Queen her role was "a vital one in the preservation of the peace of the world". Her Majesty left on 7 October for Lexington for a private visit to Kentucky and Wyoming.

Though she marked her sixtieth birthday (celebrated quietly) in 1986, Her Majesty showed no sign of slowing the pace of her state visits or trips to her realms and other countries of the Commonwealth. The Queen's 1985 Caribbean tour took her to ten countries and lasted twenty-six days. It began in Belize, one of her realms she had not previously visited, and included the Commonwealth Heads of Government meeting in the Bahamas. The year 1985 also saw the Queen in New Zealand. A twenty-two day tour of Australia took the Queen there in April and May of 1988 for the country's huge bicentennial celebration. And in March 1989 the Queen was present for the 350th anniversary of the Barbados Parliament.

It was a great help however that her children took on an increasing share of Commonwealth tours. People of every country were eager to see the Prince and Princess of Wales or the Duke and Duchess of York in person. In recognition of Princess Anne's seventeen-year role as President of the Save the Children Fund, hard work that had frequently taken her to many out of the way parts of the Commonwealth, the Queen created her only daughter Princess Royal, the seventh daughter of a sovereign to be given the title, on 13 June 1987. The year of her sixtieth birthday was the last year the Queen rode Burmese at her birthday Trooping the Colour in London. Beginning the following year she rode in a tiny carriage of Queen Victoria's. The reason for the change was security. Burmese was retired to Windsor where she died in 1990.

In October 1988 Her Majesty became the first monarch of her line and first Commonwealth sovereign to visit Spain. She spent three days in Madrid and went to Seville, Barcelona and Majorca but also managed to have some family time with her cousins King Juan Carlos I of Spain and Queen Sofia. Of all the Queen's state visits of the '80's, the one the public found most exotic was her 1987 trip to China.

On the Great Wall of China during the Queen's most memorable state visit of the '80's.

China's recent decades of isolation as an ultra-Communist dictatorship, as much as the antiquity of Chinese civilisation, made that land seem a forbidden world. This changed with the death of Mao Zedong in 1976.

The new Chinese leadership sought to open their country to the outside. An agreement with the United Kingdom in 1984 about the reversion of Hong Kong to Chinese sovereignty removed the major issue between China and the Queen's senior realm. A visit by the Queen was desired by the Chinese as recognition of their acceptance by the world community. Before embarking on this breakthrough tour, the Queen did her homework, learning as much as possible about China, even how to use chopsticks. The Chinese media in turn prepared their people for the visit and the Queen's picture was everywhere. How they saw the Queen was a lesson to the rest of the world about her international stature. Elizabeth II, according to the Chinese, possessed the virtues of the ideal Confucian Emperor. She "has behaved correctly, cautiously and devoted herself to her duty" they said. "She is sedate, gentle and knows her own mind". Chinese articles on the Queen's genealogy traced her descent from the Tang Dynasty of Chinese Emperors.

The Queen arrived Sunday, 12 October, at Shoubu Airport near Peking. Besides the Chinese Foreign Minister and other officials, she was met by about a hundred journalists. This was unusual because there were strict rules limiting the number of foreign journalists allowed to

Children wearing paper horses welcome the Queen at Shanghai in China.

enter the country. For Her Majesty's visit this limit was waived because she was Queen of so many countries. The official welcome to China took place next day in Tian An Men Square which could hold several million people and was filled for the occasion. President Li formally welcomed her at the Great Hall of the People and after a tea ceremony took her on a tour of the Forbidden City, the home of Emperors of China for five hundred years.

By request of the Queen, the menu for the banquet in the Great Hall had been reduced from seventeen courses to six. It included a dish called Buddha Leaps Over the Fence and a fruit named Dragon's Eyes. Next day Deng Xiaoping, 82, the Chinese strongman, thanked the Queen "for coming to see an old man". Her Majesty's present for Deng in the exchange of gifts was a ventilator to help his congested lungs. The Queen and Duke visited the Great Wall of China at Badaling, walking for almost a mile along it to enjoy the view of the mountains, and leaving the ever present journalists panting with the effort to catch up. Visits to Shanghai, China's largest city, Xian the ancient capital in the centre of the country, Kunming in the southwest which in World War II had been an Allied base and the end of the Burma Road, and Canton where the Queen joined thousands of youngsters at the Children's Palace, followed.

The Queen described her stay in China as "most exhilarating" and said she had been "fascinated and excited". *Britannia* sailed down the Pearl River for several days in the South China Sea before arriving at Hong Kong on 21 October. Her main job there was to reassure the anxious population about the future. Writing about the China tour, historian John McLeod said it "demonstrated once again that a monarch can bring more good will than all the Presidents and Prime Ministers in the world".

For the thirty-third anniversary of the Queen's Accession in 1985, the Canadian Government commissioned Yousuf Karsh, who first photographed the Queen as Princess Elizabeth in 1943, to take five official photographs . That year, on 31 August 1985, without anyone noticing the fact, Elizabeth II became the longest reigning monarch of Canada since Confederation in 1867. She had reigned one day longer than Queen Victoria from Confederation to her death in 1901. A brief constitutional storm blew up when the Secretary of State, David Crombie, issued proposals for a change in the Canadian Citizenship Oath. One of the options was to remove the Queen. The idea originated with federal civil servants, mind-locked in the demonstrations of 1964 in

Quebec, which they saw as proof that the Queen was divisive. In reality, Canadians might be divided over what form of government their country should have but, on that occasion in 1964 as on every other during her reign, the Queen had been both symbol and champion of national unity. Public reaction to diluting the Citizenship Oath was not positive. Even those hostile to the Crown felt it was shoddy for a Minister of the Crown from a political party whose constitution pledged support for the Monarchy to be introducing measures against the Queen. The proposals were soon dropped and the Minister retired from the Cabinet.

As a farmer herself, the Queen enjoyed her visit to the grain farm of Grant Rennie at Westberry, Saskatchewan, on her 1987 stay in the province.

On 9 October 1987 the Queen arrived in Victoria. She was to attend the Heads of Government meeting in Vancouver. Forty-five Commonwealth governments were present in the British Columbia capital to grapple with perennial problems such as South Africa and new ones like Fiji where a military coup motivated by racism had just taken place. The Fiji upheaval

Walkabout during the Queen's 1987 Quebec visit.

was the first time the Queen's sovereignty had been ended by force rather than constitutional means. A statement issued on her behalf said "Her Majesty is sad to think that the ending of the Fijian allegiance to the Crown should have been brought about without the people of Fiji being given their opportunity to express their opinion on the proposal".

At the Law Courts in Vancouver on 15 October, the Queen signed a royal warrant granting an honourable augmentation to the coat-of-arms of British Columbia. At the end of the Conference she flew to Saskatchewan. In Regina the Queen unveiled a plaque marking the seventy-fifth anniversary of the opening of the Legislative Building by her great-great uncle, His Royal Highness the Duke of Connaught, Governor-General of Canada. From the Legislative Chamber Her Majesty spoke in a television broadcast to Saskatchewan students. The tour took the Queen and Duke to Saskatoon and four centres in the east-

ern part of the province. In western Saskatchewan the Queen paid a leisurely visit to the grain farm of Grant Rennie at Westberry.

The crucial part of this tour however was the visit to Quebec, the first specific Quebec visit since 1964. The ideological fervour of separatism had recently declined and the Canadian Government of Brian Mulroney successfully negotiated an agreement with the provincial premiers in the spring called the Meech Lake Accord. The object of the Accord was to make Quebec, which had not agreed to the changes in the revised constitution proclaimed by the Queen in 1982, feel once more morally and symbolically part of Confederation. The visit was to help Robert Bourassa, Premier of the province, in demonstrating the reality of this settlement to his own people and the rest of Canada.

At the provincial dinner given by Robert Bourassa, Premier of Quebec, 22 October 1987. The Queen and Bourassa were hopeful about Quebec's re-integration in Confederation and beginning a new chapter in its relationship with the Crown.

The Queen was greeted by Gilles Lamontagne, Lieutenant-Governor of Quebec, and the Premier, Robert Bourassa, when she landed at Quebec Airport 21 October. She stayed at the Citadel, her official residence, where the Governor-General awaited her. Next day Her Majesty and the Duke of Edinburgh visited Rivière-du-Loup and La Pocatière, two towns downstream on the St Lawrence of which they had happy memories from the 1951 tour. At Rivière-du-Loup, the Queen dedicated Place de la reine Elizabeth II and did a walkabout, being warmly greeted by about 2,000 people.

In the evening, the Queen was the guest of the Premier at a dinner in the restaurant of the National Assembly. Replying in French to the Premier's toast she said that "the Constitutional Accord of 1987 recognises that Quebec constitutes a distinct society" and praised the Prime Minister and all the Premiers for their achievement in producing it. Brian Mulroney gave a dinner in the Queen's honour at the Chateau Frontenac on the eve of her departure. Here again, before 400 guests, Her Majesty referred to the Meech Lake Accord. It was she said "the culminating point [of the constitutional process] on the relations which would forthwith exist within this Confederation". Everyone agreed the Quebec visit was a great success—a resumption of the two centuries of rapport between the Crown and its French-speaking Canadian subjects. It had challenged the indifference that had settled over Quebec as the bitterness of separatism subsided. This development reflected satisfaction with the constitutional agreement.

Though the Queen had only voiced support for the general approach of the Meech Lake Accord and had not commented on any specific clauses, she was pointedly criticised for her remarks by its opponents. Her action however had been perfectly constitutional. She was simply exercising her well-known right to encourage her Ministers. The Accord moreover had widespread support, not only of the national government but from all ten premiers. The Queen

Official welcome to Canada and Alberta, Olympic Plaza, Calgary, 27 June 1990. People had been waiting as long as eight hours in the heat to see the Queen.

always supports her Governments. Even when the Trudeau Government asked for a letter from her at the time of Bill C-60 to strengthen its hand, she responded, though since only one sentence was made public it must have been a frank communication.

During the 1987 tour, the Canadian Government promised to send 110 maple trees to the Queen for creation of groves at Windsor and Balmoral. In April the following year they fulfilled this pledge when the trees were dispatched by Hercules transport planes. The Queen received Brian Mulroney on her official birthday 23 May 1988 at the Palace as he began a six day trip to European countries. In the summer native leaders left a letter for Her Majesty at the Palace requesting "Her Majesty the Queen ... to join us in protection of our sacred treaty rights". They were involved in a dispute with the federal government over education, claiming treaties provided for post-secondary education when Ottawa said they only applied to primary. In 1988 the Queen issued Royal Letters Patent allowing the Governor-General to constitute a body to exercise the royal prerogative in matters of heraldry in Canada. Underminers of the Crown in the Ottawa civil service made this look as though the Sovereign were surrendering her powers. That is not what the Letters Patent said. The Canadian Heraldic Authority, the body being created, would exercise "all powers and authorities lawfully belonging to us as Queen of Canada in respect of the granting of armorial bearings in Canada". The powers remained the Queen's.

During the bitter Goods and Services Tax debate that ended in 1990, the Queen was once more called on to make Canadian history. She became the first Monarch to give permission under Section 26 of the Constitution Act 1867 to the government to create extra members of the Senate of Canada. The Mulroney Cabinet needed extra Senators to obtain a majority in the appointed upper house where the Liberals were numerically stronger. This power allows the Crown to overcome a constitutional log jam in favour of the democratically elected House of Commons. It is such an important and

extraordinary one that it was specifically entrusted to the Monarch herself as the ultimate constitutional authority.

The Queen of Canada entered the '80's to echoes of Bill C-60 and found constitutional issues along the way throughout the decade. It was not suprising they accompanied her into the '90's too. She arrived in Calgary for her 1990 tour on 27 June, just a week after the failure of the Meech Lake Accord. At the provincial luncheon, she was presented with a gift from

Arriving on Parliament Hill for Canada Day, the 123rd anniversary of Confederation, 1 July 1990. The Queen's 1990 tour came a week after the failure of the Meech Lake Accord and had a calming effect, reassuring Canadians about the future. "I am not a fair weather friend" declared the Queen "and I am glad to be here at this sensitive time".

The Queen arrives at the Library of Congress for a luncheon on her 1991 state visit to the United States.

the city of Red Deer, the Queen Elizabeth II Scholarship in Pediatrics and Neonatology. On the same occasion, the Premier, Don Getty, announced she had given the designation Royal to the provincial paeleontological museum at Drumheller—only the third Canadian museum to receive such an honour.

At the Spruce Meadows Equestrian Centre outside Calgary, the Queen presented prizes at the first running of the Queen Elizabeth II Cup. In the afternoon she visited members of the Treaty 7 Nations represented by six bands, the Chiniki, Bearspaw, Goodstoney, Bloods, Peigans and Sarcees. She also received the gift of a 4-year-old locally bred Hanoverian gelding named Wigwam. At the provincial dinner 29 June the Queen touched on the political situation. "When Canada has faced political stresses and strains, or the threat of internal divisions, I

have followed the events with anxiety and deep concern, and with prayers and hopes that those problems can be resolved" she said.

Next day as Colonel-in-Chief of the Calgary Highlanders, Her Majesty presented them with a new Queen's colour at McMahon Stadium before 35,000 people. That night she arrived quietly in Ottawa for Canada Day, the 123rd anniversary of Confederation. Her presence in the capital helped ease the tension of months of wrangling about Meech Lake and diverted the attention of Canadians to the more positive aspects of the nationhood they shared. On Sunday, 1 July, after spending the night at Rideau Hall, the Queen drove to Parliament Hill where over 40,000—four times the normal crowd for the annual celebration—had gathered by the time she arrived at 11:00 a.m.

In his speech of welcome, the Prime Minister told the Queen "Your Majesty's selfless commitment to the cause of Canada's unity and your deep personal understanding both of our promise and our problems explains why Your Majesty is held in such admiration and affection by so many millions of Canadians". In reply the Queen spoke frankly about the current situation. It was a united Canada she first visited as Princess in 1951 and became Queen of in 1952, and had got to know so well, she said, and it was that Canada she trusted she would see in future years when she came again. Then in words that by their simple sincerity moved millions across the land, she declared: "I am not just a fair weather friend, and I am glad to be here at this sensitive time". She hoped her presence might call to mind "those many years of shared experience, and raise new hopes for the future". The

Queen also offered a definition of the Crown. "Our ceremony here today brings together Sovereign, Parliament and people—the three parts of Constitutional Monarchy. That is a system in which those who represent the community come together to reconcile conflicting interests. It is a system that has worked well for a long time." The Queen left that day for London and a summit of world leaders.

The period from the Silver Jubilee to the beginning of the '90's was on the whole one of fulfilment for Elizabeth II. She was a respected world figure, a monarch of experience, skill and wisdom. She had come to know her Canadian kingdom especially well. In her family life, three of her four children had married and she had the pleasure of seeing three sets of grandchildren born and growing up. In her own married life she clearly remained very happy. If any decade was her golden age perhaps the '80's deserve the title. Whatever reserves of strength and resolve she stored up in these fruitful years would be sorely needed as she approached an era of great trial, a period ominously heralded by the announcement of the separation of the Princess Royal and Captain Mark Phillips in 1989.

The Queen and Duke of Edinburgh with President George Bush and his wife Barbara in the White House garden 1991.

THE QUEEN AND THE NATIVE PEOPLES

Throughout the history of Canada the Crown has maintained a special relationship with the native peoples of the country and the Queen has continued this association all during her life and reign.

On the 1951 tour of Canada by Princess Elizabeth and the Duke of Edinburgh they received a gift box from an aboriginal chief and his wife.

In Calgary in 1951 five southern Alberta tribes set up a special village of 1500 people at the exhibition grounds for the royal couple to inspect.

In 1959 another village was set up in Nanaimo on Vancouver Island for the now Queen and Duke to visit. This time the arrangements were made by the Salish tribe.

The communion silver given by Queen Anne is now shared by the Tyendinaga Mohawk Territory at Deseronto, Ontario and the Six Nations Mohawk Territory near Brantford, Ontario. The chalice in the front was a gift from Queen Elizabeth II in 1984 to replace a piece that was lost.

A portrait of No Nee Yeath Taw No Row by John Verelst. He was one of the four Mohawk Kings received by Queen Anne in London in 1710. As a result of their visit the Queen sent communion silver to the Mohawks of North America, which was brought by them to Canada from New York State after the American Revolution. The Queen was present when the series of four paintings, which hung for many years at Hampton Court Palace, was received by the National Gallery of Canada in 1977.

In 1984 the Queen visited the Six Nations Mohawk Territory. The two Mohawk territories are also home to the two Mohawk Royal Chapels, among only a very few royal chapels in the Commonwealth.

In 1990 the Queen greeted members of Treaty 7 aboriginal territories at Calgary's Spruce Meadow's Equestrian Centre.

At Buckingham Palace in June 1976 the Queen welcomed Indian Chiefs and their wives. The visit celebrated treaties of 1876 and 1877 between the Crown and Saskatchewan and Alberta tribes.

The Queen speaks to aboriginal leaders at Prince George, British Columbia in 1994.

At the 1997 Aboriginal Cultural Festival in the Northwest Territories, the Queen held one of her many meetings with aboriginal Canadians of the North. At the event, Bill Erasmus (seated, second from left) asked Her Majesty to help settle the Dene treaty disputes.

9

Fin de Siècle

1992–2000

The Ruby Jubilee of the Queen's accession to the Throne was celebrated on 6 February 1992. Unlike silver, golden or diamond jubilees, ruby jubilees (marking fortieth anniversaries) are not officially recognised celebrations, so there was to be no year of festivities as there had been in 1977. There were some observances to mark this milestone however. In London the British Prime Minister, the Rt Hon. John Major, and the Leader of the Opposition gave statements of congratulations in the House of Commons. In Canada a private member, William VanKoughnett introduced a motion of congratulation which was passed by the Commons. A Royal Anniversary Trust was established in the United Kingdom, with money coming from the private sector. A new video on the life of the Queen, *Elizabeth R*, was released, and numerous organisations throughout the Commonwealth arranged observances of various kinds.

The major ceremonial commemoration came from the Commonwealth. To mark the Queen's fortieth anniversary as Head of the Commonwealth, Her Majesty was presented with the Commonwealth Mace. One hundred and five-cm long and weighing five kilos, it was made of eighteen carat gold from Wales and around the Commonwealth. The head of the mace was a large, oval ruby,

The Commonwealth Mace was the gift to Her Majesty from her "Family of Nations" to mark her Ruby Jubilee on the Throne.

surmounted by the Queen's Royal Arms of the United Kingdom, her senior realm. The staff was covered by enamel flags of each of the fifty Commonwealth countries. The mace was for use at appropriate ceremonial occasions.

In addition the Commonwealth gave Her Majesty fifty gold-plated goblets, each depicting the royal or state arms of one of the Commonwealth countries. These items were on display from the 3 April to 13 September and were presented to Her Majesty on 26 October in a ceremony televised worldwide.

On 10 February it was announced that a memorial to the Canadians who fought in the two world wars defending Great Britain, would be erected near Buckingham Palace at Green Park. On 25 February Canada was again in the news when the Canadian government announced that a revamped Victoria Cross would be established by Her Majesty as the premier decoration for military bravery in the Canadian Honours System. The original Victoria Cross, established by Queen Victoria, the Mother of Canadian Confederation, had been the senior award for Canadians since it was established in 1856. No awards had been granted in over forty years however, as Canada had not been at war since Korea in 1953, until the brief Gulf and Kuwait War in 1991. Successive governments had not made an official decision on military honours after they began establishing civilian ones separate from Britain in 1967. The Gulf War had brought the question to the fore again and government officials made plans for new Canadian military decorations which did not include the Victoria Cross. The Prime Minister of Canada, Rt Hon. Brian Mulroney stepped in over the heads of his civil servants to promise

the Victoria Cross would be retained and, after months of discussion, the result was a victory for the Monarchy. The Victoria Cross was reconstituted by the Queen as part of the new Canadian military decorations and could be awarded in "police actions" by the military as well as all out war, as long as the individual honoured was under fire from hostile forces. In this it was a return to the nineteenth century qualifications for the V.C., when the British Army policed the Empire.

In the first month of 1992 the Queen had also already paid a state visit to France. It was her first trip to the country in twenty years and the third in her reign. Later, in October, she would pay her first royal visit to a united Germany, created after the fall of the Berlin Wall, when she emphasised the European focus of modern Britain. "We British are Europeans", she would declare.

All in all it had been a good start to the Ruby Jubilee for the Queen. It wasn't to last.

Before the year was out the Royal Family was hit by, or inflicted upon themselves, one crisis or bad news story after another. The Duke and Duchess of York announced their separation. The Princess Royal's divorce from Captain Mark Phillips was finalised. The marital problems between the Prince and Princess of Wales became public knowledge as taped telephone conversations of both of them, neither of which showed them in a favourable light and both of which exposed their marital woes, were revealed in the media.

Then came a book on the Princess of Wales by Andrew Morton, which delved further into the Wales's problems and caused a sensation. In later years it was revealed by Morton that the Princess had in fact assisted him with the book.

On 9 December the British Prime Minister announced in the House of Commons that the Prince and Princess of Wales had separated.

But the problems were not limited to matrimonial. On the 20 November, the forty-fifth anniversary of the Queen and Duke of Edinburgh's wedding, a fire broke out in Windsor Castle during renovations. Soon a large part of the public rooms, including the magnificent St George's Hall, was engulfed in flames and destroyed. When it was suggested by the government that it would pay for the restoration of the Castle, there was an outcry from segments of the public who demanded that the Queen pay for it out of her own funds. On 26 November the Queen announced that she would begin paying income tax on her private income and reduce the number of members of the Royal Family who would receive allowances from the Civil List for public duties.

In addition, earlier in the year, on 10 March, Mauritius, one of the Queen's independent realms, became a republic. At the end of the year, on 17 December, the Australian government of republican Paul Keating announced that the Queen would be dropped from the Australian citizenship oath.

On 24 November at the Guildhall in London, the Queen's Ruby Jubilee was honoured by the City of London at a luncheon in the historic dining hall. The Queen spoke to her listeners in the room, and around the Commonwealth, about the experience she had been through in 1992. Her words became the media "sound bite" of the year—the *Annus Horribilis*—and one of her most remembered speeches.

A devastating fire at Windsor Castle on 20 November 1992 symbolised the year that was known as the "annus horribilis".

1992 is not a year I shall look back on with undiluted pleasure. In the words of one of my more sympathetic correspondents, it has turned out to be an '*Annus Horribilis*'. I suspect that I am not alone in thinking it so. ...

A well-meaning bishop was obviously doing his best when he told Queen Victoria, 'Ma'am, we cannot pray too often, nor too fervently, for the Royal Family.' The Queen's reply was 'Too fervently, no; too often, yes.' I, like Queen Victoria, have always been a believer in that old maxim 'moderation in all things'. I sometimes wonder how future generations will judge the events of this tumultuous year. I dare say that history will take a slightly more moderate view than that of some contemporary commentators.... After all, it has the inestimable advantage of hindsight. But it can also lend an extra dimension to judgement, giving it a leavening of moderation and compassion—even of wisdom— that is sometimes lacking in the reactions of those whose task it is in life to offer instant opinions on all things great and small....

No institution—City, Monarchy, whatever—should expect to be free from the scrutiny of those who give it their loyalty and support, not to mention those who don't. But we are all part of the same fabric of our national society and that scrutiny, by one part of another, can be just as effective if it is made with a touch of gentleness, good humour and understanding....

Forty years is quite a long time. I am glad to have had the chance to witness, and to take part in, many dramatic changes in the life of this country. But I am glad to say that the magnificent standard of hospitality given on so many occasions to the Sovereign by the Lord Mayor of London has not changed at all. It is an outward symbol of one other unchanging factor which I value above all— the loyalty given to me and my family by so many people in this country and the Commonwealth, throughout my reign.

You, my Lord Mayor, and all those whose prayers—fervent, I hope, but not too frequent —have sustained me through all these years, are friends indeed.

It was a remarkable speech, which revealed not only the Queen's sense of vulnerability to criticism, fair and unfair, which clearly hurt her, but also her resolve to face the critics head on. Implicit in the speech for those who knew the Queen's approach to problems, whether Her Majesty intended it or not, was the fact that the Queen had usually tempered her scrutiny of others with the "touch of gentleness, good humour and understanding" that she was not receiving in return from so many.

The year, bad as it was, was not without its positive side. The Queen's tour of Canada certainly fit into the category of a success. It provided a needed break of sunshine in the middle of a rather bleak year.

There was a two-fold purpose to the tour. 1992 was the 125th anniversary of Confederation and the Queen would preside at the national celebrations in Ottawa, and the Canadian Parliament had voted in 1990 to erect a statue in honour of the Queen and it was now ready to be unveiled in celebration of her Ruby Jubilee. It was a short trip but one long on

The Queen's 1992 tour of Canada was a break of sunshine in a bleak year. The Queen unveiled a statue of herself on Parliament Hill on 30 June to mark her Ruby Jubilee and also inaugurated a stained glass window in Rideau Hall for the anniversary.

warmth and significance. The Queen arrived on 30 June and unveiled the equestrian statue of herself on Parliament Hill. It flanked the east side of the Centre Block of Parliament as the statue of Queen Victoria flanked the west side, symbolising the parallel roles of two great monarchs—both women—in Canada's history. The Queen was depicted riding astride Centenial, the Royal Canadian Mounted Police horse given to the Queen in 1973. After the ceremony, attended by thousands on Parliament Hill, the Queen unveiled two stained glass windows at Rideau Hall, one marking the fortieth anniversary of her reign, the other the fortieth anniversary of the appointment of the first Canadian-born Governor-General. She also presented new colours to her regiment, the Canadian Grenadier Guards.

The next day, 1 July, Canada Day in the Dominion, the Queen presided over the swearing in of new members of the Queen's Privy Council for Canada, then presided over the celebrations on Parliament Hill as a crowd of thousands gathered for the second day in a row before their Queen. The Prime Minister, Rt Hon. Brian Mulroney paid tribute to Her Majesty in his speech: "The Crown has symbolised a continuity in the values of decency, fairness and equality before the law that have made this country great. And no Sovereign has served her Canadian subjects with more grace, more concern, and more goodwill than has Queen Elizabeth II. The Queen's sense of duty, her courage, warmth and her humour are known and appreciated by all Canadians. You have stood, Your Majesty, with Canadians and you have stood by them, and Canadians in turn regard you with loyalty and affection. Here you are truly at home and we are honoured that you have chosen to be with us on this 125th anniversary of Confederation."

In her reply, the Queen spoke of the need for Canadians to serve their country: "The real Constitution is not cast immutably on the printed page but lives in the hearts of the people. I ask them [the elected representatives] to think first

and foremost of the national interest—Canada's interest. … You have inherited a country uniquely worth preserving. I call on you all, wherever you may live, whatever your walk of life, to cherish this inheritance and protect it with all your strength."

By the end of 1992 the glow of those days in Ottawa must surely have faded in consideration of what followed, but they still stood as a reminder of the enduring value and role of the Crown throughout even the greatest troubles.

The *Annus Horribilis* was not the only year in the nineties to witness trouble for the Royal Family. More was to follow and the fortunes of the Royal Family waned and waxed, not only in Britain but in other parts of the Commonwealth, and not always at the same time. On at least one occasion, support for the Monarchy went up in Canada while it was going down in the United Kingdom. Beginning in 1993 however, the Queen and the Royal Family undertook a campaign, not so much to reinvent the Monarchy,

1992 was also the 125th anniversary of Confederation and, on 1 July, the Queen presided at Canada Day festivities on Parliament Hill, accompanied by the Governor-General, Rt Hon. Ray Hnatyshyn, and cut a birthday cake in Confederation Park.

as to reassess and redirect its role and energies at the end of the century. The greatest shock to come to the institution, however, was not even anticipated in 1992 by any observer, nor could it have been.

The late winter and spring of 1993 brought the formal separation of the Duke and Duchess of York on 28 January and the Royal Family began to define itself in a narrower sense. The Duchess remained a controversial figure in the royal circle however, condemned by many, admired by some, held in affection by others who were still her critics, and loved by her estranged husband, the Duke of York, and their children. This division in people's attitudes was reflected among the other members of the Royal Family as well, and the Queen had to negotiate her way through these conflicting personal and political shoals.

On 4 March the Queen's honours system in Britain was remodelled. It had grown organically over the decades and centuries, becoming in the process more complex and, occasionally, incomprehensible to ordinary people. The changes introduced were, in some ways, equally exotic, but essentially the purpose was to open up the honours not exclusively in the Queen's personal gift (that is, those awarded on advice), to greater public involvement. In other words to make the honours, and thus the Monarchy, more democratic. Now the general public could nominate individuals for honours through nomination forms, as was already the case in Canada and other parts of the Commonwealth.

The fall was equally eventful for the Queen. As in Australia the previous fall, in Canada attacks began once again on the place of the Queen in the Canadian Oath of Citizenship.

And on 18 September, Paul Keating told the Queen in an audience at Balmoral Castle that he intended to turn Australia into a republic by the end of the century. He also invited the Prince of Wales to tour the country the next year.

On 19 October the Commonwealth Conference was held in Nicosia, Cyprus. When the Queen arrived she became the first of her line to go to Cyprus since Richard I, The Lionheart. At the Conference the Commonwealth voted to re-admit South Africa after the country held its first multi-racial elections in April of the following year, now that the system of apartheid had ended. The hopes of the 1961 Conference which adopted the Canadian Prime Minister, John Diefenbaker's position on racial equality, that South Africa would one day concur and rejoin the family, were about to be realised. A perennial thorn in the Commonwealth's side was being removed. Regrettably the people of South Africa did not get to revote on whether the country should be a monarchy. When the republic was originally established the black population, the great majority in the country, was not allowed to vote, so the country had never democratically rejected the Crown.

Windsor Castle partially reopened to the public on 4 January 1994 (not the damaged part which would take a few more years to restore) which was good news. The Queen also undertook a three-week tour of the Commonwealth Caribbean from 18 February to 10 March. The highly successful tour included eight countries—Anguilla, Dominica, Guyana, Belize, Cayman Islands, Jamaica, Bahamas and Bermuda, all part of the Queen's realms except Guyana and Dominica. The Crown was back on track.

A three-week Caribbean tour in February and March of 1994 included an inspection of a guard of honour in Nassau on 6 March.

This was reinforced by the fiftieth anniversary of D-Day celebrations on 6 June in which the Queen and her family played a highly visible role. The Queen, the Duke and the Queen Mother in particular were the only leaders present who were also notable figures during the war in the public's mind.

At Gold Beach in Normandy, France, rank after rank of British veterans marched past the Queen and Royal Family to the old marches and wartime songs, the Queen singing along with them. The spirit of King George VI was there too and the ghosts of the multitude of Commonwealth soldiers who had fought on D-Day and elsewhere for King, Commonwealth, Empire and Country.

Three days before, the Queen, accompanied by most of the Royal Family, all colonels-in-chief of Canadian regiments, unveiled the Canada Memorial at Green Park just outside Buckingham Palace, the memorial that had been announced in 1992. The Queen Mother (the wartime Queen), the Duke of Edinburgh, the Duke of York in the uniform of the modern Canadian Forces, the Princess of Wales, Princess Margaret, the Duke of Kent and Princess Alexandra were all present.

The memorial to those Canadians who were based in Britain and defended that sceptred isle in the two world wars, was built on a line running from the Palace to Halifax, from whence the Canadians had sailed. But the memorial not only linked Halifax to the Palace but all Canadians as well, and the ceremony linked the generations of Canada's Royal Family as it did the generations of the whole Canadian family. For Canadians it put the Royal Family back into focus as the centre of Canadian society, in anticipation of the Queen's August tour of the Dominion that was imminent.

Then the Crown received a setback on 29 June when an interview of the Prince of Wales with Jonathan Dimbleby was broadcast. While the vast majority of the interview was positive, the Prince admitted to adultery and that was what the public focused on. And His Royal Highness's other remarks were taken out of context or distorted to increase the damage. Again the Queen found herself on the defensive.

Once again Canada provided a change from the problems in the United Kingdom, The 13 to 22 August tour of the North American kingdom was described by tour organisers and observers

The Queen on a walkabout with the Prime Minister, Rt Hon. Jean Chrétien, outside St Paul's Anglican Church, Halifax on 13 August 1994. The church is a royal foundation, established by the Queen's great-great-great-great-great-great-grandfather, King George II.

as perhaps one of the best tours ever. It included the Maritime province of Nova Scotia, the west coast province of British Columbia and the Northwest Territories. The Nova Scotia portion of the tour took the Queen to the capital of Halifax and the historic Fortress of Louisbourg, a landmark of Canada's French royal heritage, on Cape Breton. One of the more unusual acts of the Queen was the addition of a couple of stitches to the Fort Anne Heritage Tapestry,

illustrating four centuries of the community of Annapolis Royal's history. The Canadian Minister of Heritage, Michel Dupuy, joked that it would be the most difficult thing the Queen would have to do while in Canada and Her Majesty agreed. "Easily. I can't see and I can't sew", she replied, "I don't do tapestry".

In Victoria, British Columbia the Queen and Duke were not only at home amongst Canadians but also the Commonwealth family as Her

Her Majesty enjoys lawn bowling events at the 1994 Commonwealth Games in Victoria, British Columbia.

Majesty opened the Commonwealth Games. In addition to opening the Games, which included South Africa for the first time in thirty-three years, the Queen carried out a number of engagements as Queen of Canada. She invested the Lieutenant-Governor of British Columbia, Hon. David Lam, with the Royal Victorian Order, the first Canadian lieutenant-governor to be so honoured, and persuaded him to continue in office for an additional period beyond the normal five years. On 20 August the royal couple drove to Beacon Hill Park in the Chrysler automobile used on their 1951 tour for a "seniors tea" that drew more than seniors, in fact some 7,000 people of all ages. The Queen used the occasion to take the royal walkabout a step further in informality.

During the Beacon Hill walkabout the Duke of Edinburgh lifted one youngster, who had missed giving the Queen his flowers, over the crowd control barrier and pointed him towards Her Majesty. This was a signal for other children

to slip past the barriers to see their Queen. Any consternation on the part of the security people was not shared by the Queen, who smiled happily, or the Duke, who encouraged the children, calling out "Come on, come on!"

The relaxed attitude to security in Canada was explained by the veteran Royal Tour Media Co-ordinator Clement Tousignant. "The American system relies on a huge security and yet it is ineffective.... In Canada the RCMP are really professional. You can never eliminate all the risk, but they do a fantastic job.... Everybody benefits. Canadians look at the Royal Family as part of their identity and culture and you can see the Queen has been very happy."

The final three days of the tour were spent in the Northwest Territories, where the Queen dedicated the recently built Chamber of the Legislative Assembly. "The people of the North hold a special place in our memories and in our hearts", Her Majesty told the assembled guests. The Queen expressed the deep respect that the Royal Family had for the aboriginal culture and the contribution of the aboriginal people to Canada. The territory was preparing to be divided into two new territories, the western half to retain the name of the Northwest and the eastern half to become Nunavut. Nunavut is Inuit for "Our Land" and the new territory would be the first province or territory in Canada to have a majority aboriginal population. The Queen expressed her confidence that it would build on the laws and traditions of

Queen of "the true North strong and free". In the Northwest Territories the Queen met her people as Monarch both formally, at ceremonies such as at the Territories Legislative Assembly, and informally, as at the Yellowknife airport below.

the Inuit to "create a territory which is wisely administered and founded on mutual respect for others".

On 17 October the Queen undertook the first ever royal visit to Russia, at last freed from the yoke of communism, and on 25 November the Palace announced annual accounting of finances to meet continuing criticism of the cost of the Crown.

Despite the continuing problems of the Royal Family in 1995, it was not reflected in support for the Monarchy, at least not in Canada. A public opinion poll released on 3 February indicated that support for the Crown had gone up in Canada since 1993, a low point after the

Annus Horribilis. The focus of 1995 in the Commonwealth was in New Zealand however. The Queen toured the country with the Duke of Edinburgh from 2 to 10 November in conjunction with the Commonwealth Conference being held in Auckland and to give royal assent to an historic claims settlement bill regarding the

rights of Maoris within New Zealand. Another royal first was achieved on the trip as the Queen and Duke flew not via military, government or chartered aircraft but on a regularly scheduled commercial flight.

The importance of the Crown, and of the Queen herself, was commented on by the *New Zealand Herald* during the tour. The paper compared the practice of the Queen with that of her various first ministers or other Commonwealth leaders present in Auckland. "New Zealanders have seen far more of her than they will of most Commonwealth leaders barricaded and motorcaded from the public view." the paper wrote, "Were it not for her steadying, seemingly benign influence over more than forty years, how many nations might still belong to this historic, curious association?" It was a good question with, perhaps, an obvious answer.

During this year the Queen also paid her first visit to (post-apartheid) South Africa, since 1947, where she was warmly welcomed by the country's new president, Nelson Mandela and the South African people.

The royal pattern of carrying out regular duties, meeting new political challenges and family problems and fostering positive change continued throughout 1996 and the first half of 1997. On the 28 February the Prince and Princess of Wales agreed to a divorce as their ill-fated marriage came to a definite end and the world wondered what the future role of the Princess of Wales would be outside of the Royal Family but still linked to it. On 2 March Paul Keating lost power in Australia and was replaced by the monarchist John Howard. It would be Mr Howard who would oversee the constitutional conference and referendum which

Dressed in a Maori ceremonial robe, the Queen is seen in November 1995 with her New Zealand Prime Minister and the Maori Queen in Wellington after giving Royal Assent in person to a Maori land claims settlement. It was the first time Royal Assent had been given in person in New Zealand by a monarch.

In Cape Town, in 1995, Her Majesty admits Nelson Mandela to the Order of Merit, and presents him with his insignia. The order is one of the honours in the Queen's personal gift.

Mr Keating had set in motion and which would decide the fate of the Crown in Australia. Monarchists knew that it would be an even-handed fight now, as the new government included both supporters and opponents of the Monarchy, and the arrangements would not be biased. This was followed on 25 March with the Queen's first ever visit to Poland. Meanwhile, in New Zealand, the republican Prime Minister Jim Bolger was still in power and an independent honours system was established in the country on 2 May. On 16 April the divorce of the Duke and Duchess of York was finalised. On 31 May at the University of Wales in Aberystwyth, where the Prince of Wales had studied in 1969, the Queen was forced to cancel a planned visit after two hundred demonstrators made it unsafe. In a bow to Scottish nationalism, on 3 July, the British Prime Minister announced that the Stone of Scone, on which Scottish and

British monarchs had been crowned for centuries, would be returned to Scotland from Westminster Abbey, where it was currently kept under St Edward's Chair. It would be returned to the Abbey for coronations however. Some wondered if that would in fact happen. It may have seemed ironic to some when the Queen told Nelson Mandela, the President of the now multi-racial government of South Africa on his first visit to Britain, returning the Queen's visit of the previous year, that "You and your country can show a world often dominated by division that reconciliation and decency can prevail".

But the range of emotions and events that were 1996 were as nothing compared to what would be felt in 1997. It was the golden wedding anniversary year of the Queen and Duke of Edinburgh, so it was arranged that 4,000 couples, including some Canadians, from around the Commonwealth, who were also married in 1947, would be invited to a special garden party

Accompanied by Princess Maka Chakri, Her Majesty the Queen visits Chulalongkorn University during her state visit to King Bhumibol Adulyadez of Thailand in October 1996. The Queen's visit coincided with the 50th anniversary of the Thai Monarch's Accession.

at Buckingham Palace on 15 July. The main celebration of the anniversary would come of course in November.

On 24 June 1497 Giovanni Caboto, known to history as John Cabot, landed in Newfoundland and planted the banner of King Henry VII of England. Cabot's landing was the beginning of the Canadian Monarchy, as the authority exercised by the Queen began with that claim. The idea of monarchy was even older in Canada however, as many of the aboriginal peoples also had a monarchical form of government. The Royal Family have always respected and reflected this strand in the Canadian royal heritage and the special relationship between the Crown and the aboriginal peoples that flowed from it.

To mark the anniversary, the Queen and Duke of Edinburgh returned to Canada on 23 June. The next day Her Majesty, surrounded by 30,000 people, welcomed a replica of Cabot's ship, the *Matthew*, which had sailed from Bristol, recreating Cabot's historic voyage. For Canada's aboriginal peoples the anniversary was not one solely of celebration however, as they see the arrival of Europeans as also leading to an end of their own independence and much of their way of life. Some peaceful demonstrators were present in Newfoundland, led by Ovide Mercredi, National Chief of the Assembly of First Nations. While the politicians present ignored them, the Queen went over to the group and told Mr Mercredi she was glad that they had come.

The second part of the tour was to southwestern Ontario, where the Queen visited London, the expanded Stratford Shakespearean Festival theatre (founded the year of the Queen's Coronation), and the Bell homestead in Brantford, where Alexander Graham Bell conducted the first long-distance telephone call. In Toronto Her Majesty visited a Chinese-Canadian seniors' residence, the 48th Highlanders of Canada regiment, of which she is Colonel-in-Chief, and attended the Queen's Plate horse race for the third time.

The tour concluded in Ottawa, where the Queen was present for Canada Day for the third time in eight years. In her remarks on Parliament Hill, Her Majesty noted "Prince

In Bonavista Harbour, Newfoundland, on 24 June 1997, the Queen greets the crew of the replica ship Matthew, *which had recreated the epic voyage of the original ship, from which John Cabot landed in Newfoundland and claimed it for the Queen's ancestor King Henry VII. This event, 500 years before, was the beginning of the royal authority in Canada which is vested in the Queen.*

Addressing over 900 people at a dinner given by the Prime Minister, Rt Hon. Jean Chrétien, in Toronto, the Queen praised the Ontario capital as "a city which has always attracted people from the four corners of the globe", 28 June 1997.

the months between her engagement and marriage to the Prince of Wales had in 1981.

The tragedy brought almost unbearable pressure, and criticism, on the Royal Family. While most of this fell on the Prince of Wales, whom many now blamed for the situation that led to the Princess's death, much also fell on the Queen. She had to walk a narrow path between the desire of the Princess's family for privacy and the public's demand to know, to feel and to take part in everything. The Palace was engulfed in a flood of criticism and advice, often ill-considered.

To a great extent the criticism was based on two premises. First, because the Princess had been estranged from the Prince of Wales, many assumed that the Royal Family must naturally be indifferent to her fate. Secondly, because the

Philip and I have visited many, many parts of Canada over the years... The diversity of the country and the people never fails to amaze me. In that diversity there lies much strength... I urge you to make a commitment to help this wonderful nation to go from strength to strength as year succeeds year." The Queen was also invited later that afternoon to cut a cake at Lansdowne Park in front of 3,500 seniors, many chosen because they had been married for fifty years, to mark the Queen and Duke of Edinburgh's fiftieth wedding anniversary, as Canada took advantage of the royal couple's presence in the country to celebrate a few months early.

On 31 August, Diana, Princess of Wales died in a Paris car crash. Shock swept the globe. The interval between Diana's death and burial focused the world's attention just as

At Woodbine Racetrack in Toronto on 29 June 1997 the Queen arrived to see her third Queen's Plate horserace.

Her Majesty and the Duke of Edinburgh attended a Canada Day Seniors' celebration at Lansdowne Park, Ottawa, and cut a cake for an early cele-bration of their 50th wedding anniversary, 1 July 1997.

Royal Family had always conducted themselves on the basis that one did not show too much emotion in public, many assumed they felt no emotion.

In such an environment it was inevitable that the actions of the Queen and the Royal Family would be criticised. And they were. One thing was clear. The majority of the public—in Britain, in the Commonwealth, and, it seemed, in the world—embraced the expression of emotion in public to a far greater degree than they had in the past. It was irrelevant whether this was objectively good or bad, it was a fact. And

it was a fact that the Royal Family had not undergone such a change. The result was a division between how the Royal Family reacted to the death and how the public did. And no royal family can be too much out of step with its people.

The Royal Family mourned in private for the first few days. The people wanted them to mourn in public. As the Royal Union Flag never flew from Buckingham Palace, only the personal banner of the reigning monarch, no one in authority thought of flying it at half-mast. The people did not remember what had happened every other day and assumed that the policy was a slight to Diana. The Royal Family was clearly caught unawares, not by the feeling for Diana or the need for mourn-ing, but how the modern world expected it to be carried out. To address the situation the Queen spoke to her people, with compassion and with strength, on 7 September, the day before the funeral:

> Since last Sunday's dreadful news we have seen, throughout Britain and around the world, an overwhelming expression of sadness at Diana's death. We have all been trying in our differ-ent ways to cope. It is not easy to express a sense of loss, since the initial shock is often succeeded by a mixture of other feelings: disbelief, incompre-hension, anger—and concern for those who remain.
>
> We have all felt those emotions in these last few days. So what I say to you now, as your Queen and as a grand-mother, I say from my heart.

First, I want to pay tribute to Diana myself. She was an exceptional and gifted human being. In good times and bad, she never lost her capacity to smile and laugh, nor to inspire others with her warmth and kindness. I admired and respected her—for her energy and commitment to others, and especially for her devotion to her two boys. This week at Balmoral, we have all been trying to help William and Harry come to terms with the devastating loss that they and the rest of us have suffered.

No one who knew Diana will ever forget her. Millions of others who never met her, but felt they knew her, will remember her. I, for one, believe that there are lessons to be drawn from her life and from the extraordinary and moving reaction to her death. I share in your determination to cherish her memory.

In the months and years to come after the death of the Princess of Wales, the press and the public were to scrutinise and assess the efforts and success of the Queen and the Royal Family in incorporating those lessons into their activities

After the death of Diana, the Princess of Wales, the Queen and the Royal Family had to address the criticism directed their way by the public and adapt the Monarchy to the changed conditions in Britain and throughout the Commonwealth, as they have had to do throughout the Queen's reign.

and decisions. It would be a slow process of adjustment. As always, of course, so many people had divergent views of just what those lessons were and there was no clear path for the Queen to follow. Ultimately, as always, she would have to rely on her own judgement in implementing the changes she saw as necessary

In October 1997 the Queen and Duke made a state visit to Pakistan and India to mark a half-century of independence for the two Commonwealth countries.

and in adapting to the changes that others required from her.

On the 7 October the Queen and Duke began a two-week tour of Pakistan and India to mark the fiftieth anniversary of the two countries' independence when the old Indian Empire was ended. From 24 to 27 October the biennial Commonwealth Conference was held in Edinburgh and the Queen took another step forward in her role as Head of the Commonwealth. In 1973, at Ottawa, the Queen had attended for the first time outside of the United Kingdom and she attended all subsequent conferences. But her involvement had been limited to the social events and meeting her prime ministers individually. In Edinburgh, for the first time, the Queen attended the meetings and gave the opening address. And on 14 November a party for the 1500 workers who had restored Windsor Castle was held as the historic home of the Royal Family was at last fully restored and opened to the public.

The golden wedding anniversary of the Queen and Prince Philip took place on 20 November. In light of the year's events and, in particular, the death of the Princess of Wales less than three months before, the celebrations were perhaps more subdued that they might have been. But the people of the Commonwealth and the royal families of the

The Queen accepts one of many floral tributes during a walkabout after the 50ᵗʰ wedding anniversary service at Westminster Abbey.

world paid tribute to the royal couple on this special occasion. A luncheon at the Guildhall in London and a gala concert at the Royal Festival Hall were held on the nineteenth, the latter attended by over fifty members of European royal houses and 2,700 members of the public.

On the anniversary day itself there was a thanksgiving service at Westminster Abbey, featuring many of the same elements as were included in the wedding at the Abbey fifty years before. This was followed by a luncheon at the Banqueting House in Whitehall, dubbed the "people's banquet", as the Queen asked that the three hundred guests include ordinary citizens from various walks of life in addition to celebrities and politicians.

The Queen's speech at the luncheon was forthright in addressing the question of public opinion and the problems in trying to draw the correct lessons to be learnt in the wake of Diana's death. Her Majesty acknowledged that "For us, a royal family, however, the message is often harder to read, obscured as it can be by deference, rhetoric or the conflicting currents of public opinion. But read it we must. I have done my best, with Prince Philip's constant love and help, to interpret it correctly through the years of our marriage and of my reign as your Queen. And we shall, as a family try to do so in the future."

And speaking of the Duke of Edinburgh, the Queen paid him a rare public tribute: "He is

The Queen, accompanied by the Prince of Wales, arrives at the Palace of Westminster for the state opening of Parliament in the United Kingdom. As the twentieth century drew to a close the Queen encouraged the presence of her son and heir at state occasions, emphasising the continuity of the Crown into the future.

someone who doesn't take easily to compliments but he has, quite simply, been my strength and stay all these years, and I, and his whole family, and this and many other countries, owe him a debt greater than he would ever claim, or we shall ever know."

The year 1997 ended on one final sad note. On 11 December the Royal Yacht *Britannia* was decommissioned after sailing for forty-four years and one million nautical miles. She was not to be replaced. It was seen by many as another blow to the prestige of the Crown.

Certainly the *Britannia* had been a focus of Commonwealth identity as she sailed to all parts of the worldwide family, providing the only common home for their Queen shared by the various countries. She had sailed the Atlantic and the Pacific, the Mediterranean and the Baltic. She had traversed the Great Lakes of Canada and the warm waters of Australia and New Zealand. Air travel made her unnecessary perhaps, but a piece of the fabric which holds the Commonwealth together was unravelled when the *Britannia* sailed no more.

The new year of 1998 did not start any better than the old year had ended. On the 5 January it was reported that the Palace had asked the MORI polling firm to organise focus groups to consider how the Royal Family is viewed by the public and what changes could be made in the operation of the Monarchy. While there may be long term benefits to the decision, it was seen by some at the time as an act of desperation or, at least, inappropriate. Then on 14 January there was a report in the *Daily Telegraph* that Jamaica, Barbados and Belize were considering becoming republics. Although in fact nothing substantial came of these reports there were rumblings from some political quarters in the countries in that direction.

In Australia the constitutional conference, largely filled with advocates of a republic, was held from 2 to 13 February and, not surprisingly, recommended that Australia adopt a republican system with a president chosen by the Senate and House of Representatives. This was known as the minimalist approach, as its advocates said it would not really change the Australian system of government, for the new president would have essentially the same powers as the Queen. It was supported by the establishment figures in Australia but opposed by the monarchists, who understood that having a president is always a major change from having a monarch, as well as the advocates of a popularly elected president, who mistrusted the establishment and saw this type of

A pamphlet for the monarchists' side in their successful campaign in the Australian referendum on abolishing the Monarchy in favour of a republic.

republic as a grab for power by those Australian elites. Public opinion polls showed clearly that most Australians preferred either the monarch or a popularly elected president. But the "minimalists" controlled the conference and sailed ahead doggedly, like the *Titanic* into the ice field, with, ultimately, the same result for their cause. Meanwhile in New Zealand the republican Jim Bolger was replaced as Prime Minister by the monarchist Jenny Shipley in a caucus revolt over various policy differences, including the monarchy.

The year 1999, while not without its problems or criticisms for the Queen and the Monarchy, was a good year. It began with the Queen announcing on 14 January that the Queen's Gallery at Buckingham Palace was to have its display space trebled to allow the public greater access to the works of art in Her Majesty's collection. The expansion would be completed in time for the Queen's Golden Jubilee in 2002 and the development was seen as a further move to make the Monarchy itself more accessible to the public. Among the highlights for the Queen over the course of the year was the opening of the new Scottish Parliament on the 1 July. It was the first parliament in Edinburgh since the Act of Union in 1707. There was less pomp than at an opening in London, but pomp there was. The Queen rode in an open carriage from her Scottish home at Holyroodhouse Palace to the temporary Parliament building, escorted by a contingent from the Household Cavalry. In size and appearance the procession was very similar to the processions in Ottawa to the Canadian Parliament. As in Canada the security was also low-key. This led to five IRA supporters lunging at the car-

riage, though no harm came to the Queen. All along the route Her Majesty was cheered by her Scottish subjects as she has been cheered by her English, Canadian, Australian, New Zealand or Caribbean subjects when she rode to open parliaments in those lands. At the opening the Queen stood behind her Scottish Crown, clad in a purple hat and coat and tartan sash. In her remarks she said "My prayers are with you all as you embark on this new and historic journey". It was later reported that, as part of the Crown's role in the process of devolution in the United Kingdom, the Queen would spend more time living in Scotland and carrying out royal duties for the United Kingdom from Edinburgh.

On 6 November at the other end of the world the Australian people voted in the long-awaited referendum on whether Australia would remain a monarchy. The Monarchy won handily by a 55% to 45% margin, with a majority in every state. Under Australian law for a motion to pass it needed an overall majority and a majority in four of the six states. In response to the vote Her Majesty said, "I respect and accept this result. I have always made it clear that the future of the Monarchy in Australia is an issue for the Australian people and them alone to decide, by democratic and constitutional means". Some observers noted that the Queen now not only reigned in Australia by hereditary right but also by election.

The next day the Queen began a three-nation tour of Africa to reinforce Commonwealth solidarity and to open the Commonwealth Heads of Government meeting in South Africa, the first time the meeting had been held there. When the Queen and former President Nelson Mandela greeted each other the Queen said "It is good to see you. I can't tell you how nice it is to be back here". Mr Mandela said of the meeting, "I was delighted. We are old friends." While in South Africa the Queen also marked the hundredth anniversary of a less happy time, the South African War of 1899–1902, and expressed regret for the loss of life among white and black South Africans and the British, and in particular for the deaths of civilians in the British concentration camps. She rightly did not go so far as to compare them with the Nazi camps of the same name but different intent, as some Afrikaaners wished, and some staged demonstrations as a result. The other countries visited by the Queen were Ghana and Mozambique.

When the British Empire and the world celebrated the end of the nineteenth century and the dawn of the twentieth, on 1 January 1901, the event was called in French "fin de siècle". That literally meant "end of the century", but it conveyed a deeper significance as "siècle" can also mean "era, age or world". Many did see the passing of one era, and the beginning of a new one.

In the same sense, when the world celebrated the end of the twentieth century, and the dawn of the twenty-first, on 1 January 2000, many also saw the end of another era, especially as the end of a millennium, with all the portents that raised, was also celebrated. Although admitting in the House of Commons that the century and millennium would not in fact end for another twelve months, the British government said they were celebrating the Year 2000 because everyone else was, and arranged for the Queen to open the Millennium Dome

The Queen Mother prepared her daughter the Queen for her life's vocation and assisted her in fulfilling her destiny. In the year 2000 the Queen willingly took a back seat to the Queen Mother who celebrated her 100th birthday.

(constructed as the British contribution to the world-wide festivities) in London at midnight. Perhaps the false celebration symbolised the world's irrational side in a new era that had in fact already begun and had been behind much of the criticism of the Crown in the past decade. The irrational will undoubtedly remain a challenge for the Queen in the twenty-first century.

Then from 17 to 26 March of the new year, the Queen undertook her first "post-election victory" tour of Australia to visit the site of the Olympic Games in Sydney, among other venues. The Queen received a warm welcome wherever she went, one prominent republican voter even saying that having met her he now regretted that he had voted for a republic, and was glad his side had lost. The situation was still touchy enough, however, that the Australian government, led by the monarchist John Howard, did not ask the Queen to open the Games later that year but arranged for the Governor-General to do so, despite the international practice that it is always the head of state (the Queen) of the host country who performs the opening.

By August 2000 the Queen had reigned for almost half of the century that was coming to a close. One era or "siècle" had in fact been ending for the Monarchy as the years of the century passed away. It had not happened at one moment or in one way, but the change was profound. There were changes of state such as decolonisation in the new Commonwealth and nationalism in the Old Commonwealth which forced the Crown to redefine its role for each realm. There was a new spurt of democracy in the 1990s which, while not inherently at odds with monarchy, necessitated a new formula for

the exercise of power, and altered the balance of influence between the Queen's personal household, her political ministers and her people. And there was mass communication, such as the Internet, which often added to the world's information but not its understanding. It gave the world a ninety-nine year century and other rumours and false assertions, which were often believed simply because they were repeated, as well as true knowledge. It could be both dangerous and enlightening.

Human nature had always produced such dangers but the global village made the effects more pronounced and the Queen, like all public figures, continues to face a great challenge in accommodating or counteracting its effect on her role. The Queen was still treading her way through this minefield in the year 2000, balancing her role as a symbol for continuity as well as change—"the partnership of the ages" spoken of by the philosopher Edmund Burke—which has allowed the Monarchy to witness many "fins de siècles", despite the prophesies of its demise by critics.

And while the new century would not in fact begin until 2001 there was a real royal celebration in August 2000 that did mark an era, of both public and personal significance for the Royal Family. On 4 August the Queen Mother turned one hundred years old. She had been born in the last year of the nineteenth century and had lived through the entire twentieth century and into the twenty-first. It was a remarkable achievement in longevity but also in what the Queen Mother had contributed to the Commonwealth and the world in that century of life. The focus of the Commonwealth in the year 2000 was therefore not on Queen Elizabeth II but on Queen Elizabeth The Queen Mother, and the Queen consciously absented herself from the public celebration to avoid diverting any attention.

And this was appropriate. Throughout the Queen's life, regardless of the changes, good and bad, and the challenges she faced, one constant has been the steadfast support she has received from her mother. The Queen Mother gracefully moved from being her daughter's Queen to her daughter's subject and she had prepared Elizabeth II for the vocation that awaited her, then assisted her in fulfilling that destiny in a myriad of ways. As the Queen Mother's birthday approached and then was celebrated throughout the Commonwealth, and indeed the world, it was also a celebration of the strength of the Crown and the standards which King George VI and Queen Elizabeth had laid out, and which their daughter Queen Elizabeth II has always lived up to.

These standards could and did transcends centuries and millennia and provided a solid basis used by the Queen for the past half century and upon which she could draw to face the new era as she was about to mark a milestone of her own—her Golden Jubilee on the Throne.

ALL THE QUEEN'S HORSES AND ALL THE QUEEN'S DOGS

At Glamis Castle, in 1937, the eleven-year-old Princess Elizabeth exhibited her natural rapport with dogs.

While visiting the Zoological Gardens in 1937, Princess Elizabeth demonstrated an early interest in riding ponies.

The Royal Family's love of dogs, the environment in which the Princess grew up, is clearly evident in this family picture.

When her father the King was too ill to attend the 1951 King's Birthday Parade in London, Princess Elizabeth took the Sovereign's Salute on his behalf. By now she was an accomplished horsewoman. The next year she would take the Salute as Queen.

The Queen with her daughter Princess Anne, who shares her love of horses and dogs.

In 1969 the Queen was presented with Burmese, by the Royal Canadian Mounted Police. The horse became the Queen's favourite and she rode him at each Birthday Parade from 1969 through 1986.

The 60th birthday painting of the Queen and the ubiquitous corgi, by Michael Leonard. It was commissioned by READER'S DIGEST for the National Gallery. The Royal Family acquired its first corgi in 1933.

A classic image of the Queen, riding Burmese and taking the Salute at the Queen's Birthday Parade in London.

In 1987 Burmese was retired and the Queen elected to ride in a phaeton, drawn by two horses, for her Birthday Parade, rather than train another horse. With the change the scarlet uniform was also abandoned.

The Queen's rapport with dogs has not changed in the sixty-three years between the first and this recent photograph.

10

The Golden Jubilee

2001–2002

Elizabeth II became Queen in 1952. Louis St Laurent was Canadian Prime Minister, Sir Winston Churchill led the United Kingdom, Harry Truman was President of the United States and Joseph Stalin dictator of the Soviet Union. That year television was in its infancy, Britain inaugurated the first jetline air service, the Korean War raged, most women were not in the work force.

The world leaders from the start of her reign, and many who came to prominence during it, are no longer alive. The current Canadian Prime Minister (the ninth she has had), Jean Chrétien, was a teenager in 1952, the tenth British Prime Minister of her reign, Tony Blair, was not yet born, nor was Vladimir Putin, the President of the new Russia that succeeded the Soviet Union, which itself is no more. George Bush, the second of that name to be American President in the reign of Elizabeth was but a child.

The half century the Queen's reign has encompassed has witnessed tremendous changes

Canadians have known their Queen through a series of official portrait photographs taken in the fifty years of her reign. Dorothy Wilding's official photo of Princess Elizabeth, in what has been called the soft-focus, sentimental style, was the picture of Her Majesty known to countless Canadian school children in the 1950s.

225

for good and ill. One of the few constants has been the Queen and Elizabeth II stands out as a figure whose faultless devotion to duty flourishes in an age of self-gratification. Thirty years after the Canadian Prime Minister, Pierre Trudeau, predicted she would cease to be Canada's Sovereign in a decade, the Queen is preparing for the Golden Jubilee tour of her Canadian realm. Her Crown is inherited, yet after the Australian Referendum in 1999, she could add the claim of being an elected national leader. A person who feels deeply, Her Majesty shows no feeling but pleasure in public. Endowed with high spirits and a great sense of humour, she, at the same time carries out her duties with unfailing dignity and decorum.

In fifty years the Queen has also changed from a young mother of two small children, to a respected grandmother of four children, all married and three divorced, and six grandchildren, the oldest of whom are now becoming young adults themselves. She herself has matured from the inexperienced young woman who ascended the Throne.

Plans for the Golden Jubilee are taking shape. There will be a tour of Australia and New Zealand sometime in the spring. It was scheduled for the fall of 2001 but postponed after 11 September terrorist attacks on New York City that left over 5,000 dead and precipitated the world's war on terrorism. A March trip to the Caribbean is also planned. The celebrations in the United Kingdom are set for June, as they were in 1977 for the Silver Jubilee, and will once again include tours of that realm.

A Golden Jubilee Office has been established in the United Kingdom as a unit of the Department of Culture, Media and Sport. Lord Levene, a former Lord Mayor of London is heading an organising committee for events in the United Kingdom capital. He stated that Her Majesty and the British Government wished people "to do their own thing. The intention is to have a lot of spontaneous events which come from the bottom up, rather than from the top down. We want people to tell us how they want to celebrate, rather than dictate to them what somebody else wants them to do. Our job is to help coordinate operations".

Before the lengthy 1959 royal tour to open the St Lawrence Seaway, Donald McKague of Toronto was commissioned to do a series of formal photographs of the Queen of Canada at Windsor Castle.

However the government has declared that a commemorative medal for the armed forces is to be issued, that Monday 3 June will be a public holiday, with the spring bank holiday moved to 4 June from 27 May to allow for four days of public celebrations. On the fourth the Queen and members of the Royal Family will attend a national service of thanksgiving at St Paul's Cathedral, after a ceremonial procession, as also occurred in 1977 for the Silver Jubilee. The Queen will open the XVII Commonwealth Games in Manchester on 25 July and close them on 4 August. And a Golden Jubilee logo has been adopted.

The Canadian Golden Jubilee tour will be more extensive than the Silver Jubilee tour was, eleven days in October rather than just six days, and will include Ottawa and the provinces of New Brunswick, Ontario, Manitoba and British Columbia, as well as the territory of Nunavut, rather than just Ottawa, as was the case twenty-five years ago. Canada Post has also announced that it will issue a special commemorative stamp to mark the Jubilee, but, to accommodate it, will not (churlishly) issue a definitive stamp with the Queen on it for the year 2002. The postal service will thus mark the Jubilee Year by making it the first since the introduction of Canadian postage stamps in 1851 without a definitive stamp featuring either the Monarch or the Monarch's cypher.

Two of the Queen's Household Regiments, the Governor-General's Horse Guards and the

The Anthony Buckley portrait of Her Majesty was selected for the stamp issued for the Queen's momentous 1964 Canadian sojourn.

Governor-General's Foot Guards, have announced a pair of joint concerts to launch the Jubilee in February—one each in Toronto and Ottawa, their respective home cities. The Canadian Royal Heritage Trust, an educational charity charged with preserving the royal history and heritage of Canada, will be undertaking a number of Jubilee projects, including an exhibit on royal jubilees at its museum at Neustadt, Ontario in the birthplace of the Queen's second Canadian Prime Minister, John Diefenbaker.

All the celebrations will be well deserved, though, paradoxically, the outpouring of joy and the Golden Jubilee tributes will make it a year more gruelling than usual for the seventy-six year old monarch. But the anniversary points up the fact that the person and the Crown are inseparable. Some illogical people claim to like the Queen but do not care about the Monarchy. The Monarchy is what gave her peoples their Queen, without it they would never have known her.

Celebrating what the Queen has done in fifty years underlines what she is able to do. If she is worth being celebrated and supported then so must the institution which produced her and is her context. This is a lesson for her countries—Canada among them—when they toy with abandoning the Crown. The Golden Jubilee will no doubt have the effect of putting the brakes on such plans in one or two of the Caribbean countries that were recently considering it. But it is a matter that concerns the whole Commonwealth, republican as well as monarchical. Would Elizabeth II continue to be Head of the Commonwealth if she were not Queen? It is doubtful. More likely the Commonwealth as it is known would end.

Elizabeth II certainly has much to offer Canadians that they stand in need of. Service, duty, professionalism, patience, self-sacrifice, absence of rancour, belief in essential values many have lost the ability to believe in, are some of them.

Charming but definitely informal, the 1973 official Canadian portrait by Cavouk of Toronto, taken in the library of Rideau Hall 4 August 1973, has been called "the citizen Queen".

Minister of the '60's during an audience. The Queen wants her people to have the form of government and society they think is necessary and best for them. But if she is to be Queen then she is ready to give it her all. That was revealed in the hoax telephone call made by a Montreal broadcaster at the time of the second Quebec referendum in 1995. Pretending to be the Prime Minister, Jean Chrétien, this man got the Queen on the line and,

And so is putting the interests of the community ahead of self. The observation that "The Queen is the head of our nation, and our nation, as we contemplate her Headship, becomes a household itself" has lost none of its original wisdom since it was first expressed at the time of the Coronation. No other leader is as capable of creating such a sense of community.

She offers all these gifts but never seeks to impose them. From the beginning she made it clear that the Monarchy is for her people's good not her own. "Does Canada want to become a republic?" she asked Lester Pearson her Prime

discussing the question of escalating separatist support, said he wanted Her Majesty to make a national broadcast to Canadians. Send her a draft to look over was the Queen's response.

The attitude of much of the Canadian establishment to the Queen of Canada is nevertheless "The Crown, so long as it is invisible". They have made it a neglected and undervalued Canadian institution. If the official phasing out of the Queen of Canada continues, the day will come when there will be no monarchy. (A test will be whether Her Majesty is asked to open a session of Parliament on her Jubilee tour in

October 2002. If she isn't, the erosion has become serious again.) Removing her functions creates the psychology and inevitability of ending the Crown. This process has been implanted like a disease in the Canadian royal polity. Abolish the Queen say her detractors, she doesn't do anything. But she does less now because her personal role has been reduced by these very detractors. As recently as 1998, Government House suddenly dropped

Photo of Her Majesty the Queen by John Evans of Ottawa taken after she opened the 3rd Session of the 30th Parliament of Canada 18 October 1977.

Recent public awareness of the alarming ignorance and lack of teaching of Canadian history has helped. It is not possible to upgrade the importance of Canadian history without meeting the Crown at every turn. The Department of Canadian Heritage under Sheila Copps cited making Canadians aware of their identity as a constitutional monarchy as one of the objects of the

the information that the Queen is Sovereign of the Order of Canada from the regular press releases announcing appointments to the Order. When John Manley, Minister of Foreign Affairs, attacked the Crown on the Victoria weekend 2001, he said that the Queen never travels anywhere outside this country as Queen of Canada. He failed to mention that she once did—1951 (as Princess), 1957, 1959, 1961, 1984—but has since been prevented from doing so and that he is the Minister responsible for asking her to perform this role.

All the same, in Canada the Queen will not enter her Golden Jubilee year without successes. There have been signs of hope for the future.

Prince of Wales's visit in April 2001. Perhaps most surprising of all was the number of Cabinet Ministers who rushed to identify themselves as supporters of the Canadian Monarchy at the time of John Manley's attack. They included Sheila Copps, Eleanor Caplan, the Minister of Citizenship and Immigration, who said she felt proud every time she took the oath to the Queen with new Canadians, Anne McLellan, the Minister of Justice, David Collenette, Minister of Transport, Herb Gray, the Deputy Prime Minister and, of course, Jean Chrétien himself, in whose career it is not too much of an exaggeration to say the Queen has been almost like a good luck talisman.

The present Governor-General, Adrienne Clarkson, a populist in her approach, is a supporter. "Je suis monarchiste" she said in a Quebec interview. Hearing her refer to the King's Daughters (the Filles du roi were the women King Louis XIV sent to Quebec in 1654–72 as brides for settlers and soldiers) in her installation speech as Governor-General was a refreshing reminder that Canada had a history prior to 1867.

Even though the Queen is quite prepared to accept the decision of any of her realms to become a republic, she—who shows the greatest fidelity to her own word—must wonder at the integrity of public figures who swear to be "faithful and bear true allegiance" to her or even more specifically to be "a true and faithful servant to Her Majesty Queen Elizabeth II,

as a member of Her Majesty's Privy Council for Canada" and casually break it, but become incensed when separatists renounce theirs by advocating the dismemberment of the country. Ironically, though the Queen for many years has not been asked to travel abroad as Queen of Canada, she remains a well-known symbol of Canada outside the country. The picture of American gratitude that flashed around the world when the Canadian Ambassador got the American hostages in Iran freed in 1979 was "God Save the Queen!" scrawled on a bag of US mail bound for Canada. The incident of the Ovechkin family who, after being recaptured in their attempt to flee to Canada from the Soviet Union in 1988, asked a Canadian journalist if they could see a dollar, was another example. They wanted to see the picture of the Queen of Canada who symbolised the freedom they aspired to obtain but were never able to because they were killed in their next attempt.

What is it those who wish to phase the Queen out would replace her with? The *Globe and Mail's* president chosen by an Order of Canada gerontological oligarchy? A classic republic? Union with the United States? The options are not many but absorption into the United States is the most likely long term result of abolition of the Canadian Crown. Twenty-five per cent of Canadians said that they would like American citizenship in a recent survey. Because of the erosion of the Queen's role a large number of Canadians do not even know that their country is a constitutional monarchy.

Yousuf Karsh, the most famous Canadian photographer of Elizabeth II, and like Cavouk of Armenian background, did the Government of Canada's series of five official portraits for the 1980s. Karsh had first photographed Her Majesty as Princess Elizabeth in 1943.

Vincent Massey wrote that "The Monarchy is essential to us. Without it as a bastion of Canadian nationality, Canadian purpose, and Canadian independence, we could not, in my view, remain a sovereign state".

Politicians have been the only beneficiaries of transferring functions of the Queen to the Governor-General. The office of Governor-General suffered most from this process both in terms of constitutional effectiveness and national profile. Governors-General are now confused about their own role. They talk about representing the people and being part of a collective Crown (Canadian law defines the Crown not as a collective but as "the Sovereign of ... Canada") when what they represent is the Queen who is *the embodiment of the neutral state*. If Governors-General represented the people, the people would have to have a homogeneous opinion on public matters, which in reality they do not. The representatives of the people are the political leaders of the various parties. Australia's recent experience showed how hard it is to combine a presidency with a parliamentary system. Appointed presidents have no credibility whatever. People can accept an hereditary monarch or an elected president, but an elected president does not fit with a parliamentary system.

If King William IV was the first modern constitutional monarch—that is the first to practice cabinet government in which the Prime Minister's time in office depends on majority support in the Commons—then Elizabeth II is the seventh of the constitutional monarchs. Among the seven there has been only one failure—Edward VIII, who failed and quickly departed. How many institutions have such a good record?

The most recent Canadian portrait photo of the Sovereign released by the Department of Canadian Heritage on 18 June 1998 was taken at Buckingham Palace. This time the Government did not commission a Canadian to take the picture but used a Palace photographer.

But can a shared monarch work? Queen Elizabeth II is herself proof that it can. Many of her statesmen have paid tribute to her skill in keeping separate the interests of the different countries of which she is the Queen. Canada's only valid complaint about the way the shared monarch works might be that, as the largest monarchy in the world and a country of over thirty million in population, it does not get its fair share compared with the United Kingdom, a small country with a population only twice as large at some sixty million. Still Canada has received more of the Queen's time and involvement than any other of her realms except the

United Kingdom. It is hard not to conclude that in the Queen's reign the greatest tragedy for Canada has been the failure of many Canadian nationalists to see that the monarchy is potentially their greatest ally. Not only should they embrace it because it is the very reason for Canada's existence as a separate state and because having a monarch has always been Canada's nature, but also because borrowing foreign republican institutions would make Canada less Canadian.

How is it that after four decades of constant erosion of her position the Queen of Canada will be celebrating her Golden Jubilee in Ottawa, four provinces and one territory in October 2002? The best answer is given in the title of a newspaper column written by the journalist Andrew Coyne after the Queen's 1997 tour: "Everybody's against the monarchy, except the people". In fifty years on the Throne, Queen Elizabeth II has never lost the esteem and good will of the people. Her dedication, her dignity, her decorum, her deep faith in God and in people continue to find an echo in their hearts. And the natural way she carries out her duties also finds its response. Elizabeth II does not have an outgoing, exuberant personality. It is not easy for her. She knows this and does not try to put on the act of having one. Nor does she have the easy charm of her mother. Once seeing people waiting at a railway siding in New Zealand she said "If I were Mummy, I would be out there and they would adore it". Instead she behaves *naturally* by not trying to be someone else.

She *has* made a difference to the lives of Canadians. Whether it was the timber magnate H.R.MacMillan who set up graduate scholarships at the University of British Columbia in honour of her 1959 tour; the anonymous donor who—with her permission—established the Queen Elizabeth II Admission scholarship at the University of Saint Michael's College in 1998; Sister Seraphina who held the Sovereign's hand at Mundare a hundred miles north of Edmonton in 1978 and told her "I pray for you every day"; the Canadian military officer who said to the authors in 1984 "There are two women in the world I would die for—my wife and the Queen"; or the many others never heard about who were inspired to do their jobs better because of the Queen's example. From the far reaches of the North to the great cities of the south, many, many of her fellow Canadians have felt her impact.

When the Queen celebrates her Golden Jubilee in the golden glow of the Canadian autumn of 2002, perhaps she will recall that earlier autumn of 1957. It was then she quoted the words of her great predecessor, Elizabeth I, to her last Parliament: "this I count the glory of my Crown, that I have reigned with your loves" She used those words that October to frame her own wish "that in the years before me I may so reign in Canada and be so remembered". When Canadians, reasserting their identity as a royal people possessing a majestic land, offer the Queen their congratulations and show her their gratitude for fifty years of matchless service in October 2002, they will do so because that *is* how she has reigned, how she is remembered, how she is loved.